Praise for
Pastoring Worldchangers

Jason Benedict's *Pastoring Worldchangers* is a book that hits you from all directions: it equips with sound biblical teaching, challenges old, unhelpful paradigms, and inspires with fresh insight and vision. The reader will never see business, work, and entrepreneurship the same. As a pastor who at times has felt uncomfortable and unsure about how to best minister to the business community, this book is a Godsend. Each chapter left me hungry to read the next chapter!

Pastoring Worldchangers is refreshingly practical but also wonderfully prophetic, since it paints a powerful picture of what it truly looks like when the gap between Sunday and Monday is bridged. If every church leader would ingest the principles of this book, churches and communities might finally see the transformation so many long for.

>DR. DAN BACKENS
>Senior Pastor, New Life Church, Virginia Beach, Virginia
>Senior Executive Director, One Focus Network

This book is a must-read for pastors and Christian leaders. *Pastoring Worldchangers* highlights the vital role that pastors and churches must play in equipping and sending the saints into their respective assignments. Beyond pointing out what we must do, the authors provide practical wisdom on how to do this in your church.

>MARK BATTERSON
>Author and Lead Pastor of National Community Church, Washington, D.C.

Jason has done an incredible job of helping me understand how to serve God in my everyday life. His focus on equipping believers for their Monday morning assignment is exactly what I needed to hear. He's provided me with practical tools to make my work meaningful and impactful, while also reminding me to stay grounded in my faith. If you're looking for guidance on how to be an effective leader in your workplace, Jason's insights will be invaluable to you.

>JIMMY FOSTER
>Senior Pastor, River Valley Church, Herkimer, New York

Inspiring, instructional, and innovative are a few of the many transforming descriptions of this must-have resource in your leadership toolbox. Jason has compiled in one insightful book the experience of leading ministry marketplace influencers who bridge the gap between the secular and sacred divide.

With practical applications, *Pastoring Worldchangers* teaches pastors how to develop, support, equip, and activate those sitting in our pews to engage the marketplace and be the answer to the brokenness in our communities. Pastors who engage their congregations in the principles of this book will result in empowering and releasing "Worldchangers."

>DR. STEVE D. HOLDER
>President, The Fellowship Network
>Global Leadership Pastor, Bethel Church

I love this book! *Pastoring Worldchangers* by Jason Benedict is an exceptional book written to inspire and challenge those of us who minister in both the church and in the marketplace. We all have a strategic part to play. This book is written by a compilation of kingdom leaders from throughout the world who tell their inspiring stories of how the Lord is using them to expand His kingdom.

The message is clear. If you are a believer in Jesus, you are in full-time ministry. This book exposes the sacred and secular divide we find in many places today. Practical, biblical, and inspirational, *Pastoring Worldchangers* is a must-read for every pastor and church leader, and for every believer serving in the marketplace.

>Larry Kreider
>International Director of DOVE International
>Author of over 40 books

Pastoring Worldchangers

Equipping God's People for Their Monday Morning Assignments

By Jason Benedict et al.

Blessed2Bless Press

Pastoring Worldchangers
Published by Blessed2Bless Press, an imprint of Touchstone Business Solutions. Printed in the United States of America.

ISBN 978-0-9899078-6-6 (paperback edition)
ISBN 978-0-9899078-7-3 (electronic edition)

© Copyright 2023, Jason Benedict. All rights reserved, except for: Scriptures marked ERV are taken from the Holy Bible: Easy-to-Read Version (ERV), International Edition © 2013, 2016 by Bible League International and used by permission. Scripture quotations marked ESV are from The ESV® Bible (The Holy Bible, English Standard Version®), copyright © 2001 by Crossway, a publishing ministry of Good News Publishers. Used by permission. All rights reserved. Scriptures marked KJV are taken from the KING JAMES VERSION (KJV): KING JAMES VERSION, public domain. Scripture quotations marked (LEB) are from the *Lexham English Bible*. Copyright 2012 Logos Bible Software. Lexham is a registered trademark of Logos Bible Software. Scripture quotations marked MSG are taken from *THE MESSAGE*. Copyright © 1993, 1994, 1995, 1996, 2000, 2001, 2002. Used by permission of NavPress Publishing Group. Scripture quotations marked NASB taken from the New American Standard Bible® (NASB), Copyright © 1960, 1962, 1963, 1968, 1971, 1972, 1973, 1975, 1977, 1995 by The Lockman Foundation. Used by permission. www.Lockman.org. Scripture quoted by permission. Quotations designated (NET) are from the NET Bible® copyright ©1996, 2019 by Biblical Studies Press, L.L.C. http://netbible.com. All rights reserved. Scripture quotations marked (NIV) are taken from the Holy Bible, New International Version®, NIV®. Copyright © 1973, 1978, 1984, 2011 by Biblica, Inc.™ Used by permission of Zondervan. All rights reserved worldwide. www.zondervan.com. The "NIV" and "New International Version" are trademarks registered in the United States Patent and Trademark Office by Biblica, Inc.™ Scripture marked (NKJV) taken from the New King James Version®. Copyright © 1982 by Thomas Nelson. Used by permission. All rights reserved. Scripture quotations marked (NLT) are taken from the Holy Bible, New Living Translation, copyright ©1996, 2004, 2015 by Tyndale House Foundation. Used by permission of Tyndale House Publishers, a Division of Tyndale House Ministries, Carol Stream, Illinois 60188. All rights reserved. Scripture quotations marked (TLB) are taken from The Living Bible copyright © 1971. Used by permission of Tyndale House Publishers, a Division of Tyndale House Ministries, Carol Stream, Illinois 60188. All rights reserved.

Except for brief quotations in critical articles or reviews, no part of this book may be reproduced in any manner without prior written permission of the publisher: worldchangers@blessed2bless.net.

Edited by Coralie Emberson
Cover design by Sarah Benedict

Pastoring Worldchangers

Equipping God's People for Their Monday Morning Assignment

Dedication

I dedicate this book to the shepherds of God's flock everywhere. Pastors, we love you! Your labor in the Lord is not in vain. Your earnest and often heroic efforts to preach the Word to stay prepared, to correct, encourage, and patiently instruct us in truth has an impact in our lives. Never forget it.

I think of the shepherds that have led me closer to the Good Shepherd. I cherish your leadership and example in my life. I think of the thousands of pastors around the world that I have had an opportunity to meet—you are truly the salt of the earth. I think of the pastors of The Fellowship Network—I am honored to be counted among you.

My sincere prayer is that this book will encourage you, challenge you, and help you accomplish God's purposes in and through your life.

Acknowledgments

Thanks to all the contributing authors. Your encouragement and enthusiasm for this project means so much; each of your voices are needed and your patience is appreciated.

Thanks to my talented daughter-in-law, Sarah Benedict, for her beautiful cover design. You took my kernel of an idea and made it come alive with your artistry.

Thanks to my diligent and hardworking editor, Coralie Emberson. I couldn't have made it across the finish line without you.

TABLE OF CONTENTS

Dedication ix

Acknowledgments.. x

Introduction.. 1

1. Blessings and Battles, by David and Jason Benham 5
2. Loving Monday as Much as You Already Love Sunday, by Dr. Ed Silvoso 23
3. Spiritual Covering and the Symbiotic Relationship Between the Local Church and Businesspeople, by David Hodgson 37
4. Equipping Worldchangers, by Jason Benedict 59
5. Getting a Vision—Awakened to Dream, by Svetlana Papazov 77
6. Equipping Christians to Advance God's Kingdom in and Through Business, by John E. Mulford 113
7. Citywide Workplace Network, by Chuck Proudfit 129
8. Do You Want to Pastor or Transform Your City? by David Robinson 139
9. Equipping for the Other 4 C's, by Joseph Umidi 161
10. The Faith@Work Movement in America, by Os Hillman 177
11. Apostolic Economics: Building the Ecosystems of Our Cities, by James Kramer 187
12. The Birth of iWork4Him, by Jim Brangenberg............. 197
13. Two Pillars, by Paul Cuny 211

Index 227

Introduction

Pastor, imagine the setting. It's almost time for the small group to begin, and there is a knock at the door. You are standing in a comfortable living room. Most of the group is either sitting or standing around the room. There is a healthy buzz of earnest fellowship as members of the small group catch up.

The recent arrival is Hannah, an educator and successful author. You look up from your conversation with Chuck to wave at Hannah and welcome her. Chuck is the chairman of the board of a major corporation. In the corner, the two Williams are having an animated conversation. Bill, an influential politician, is laughing at something Will, a well-known math professor with political ambitions of his own, just said. Henry, a banker, steps up to take Hannah's coat.

All in all, there are 17 or 18 people present. Everyone in the room is a passionate Christian and leader of some kind—there are several ministers, a couple of educators, a handful of politicians, a lawyer, and others.

Zach looks to you and says, "Pastor, it looks like we are all here. Will you lead us in prayer to get started?"

You pray that the Lord would guide the meeting, that each of those present would be empowered by God's grace to extend His kingdom within their respective spheres of influence, that the group would be used of God to advance the gospel and heal the brokenness in the city and nation.

You invite others to pray. Some chime in and pray about poverty, the need for education, for an end to crime and human trafficking, and other issues. Zach prays for the missionaries, as always. Marianne, a single lady who seems to volunteer for everything, leads the group in a song.

As the song winds down, you ponder how amazing it is to fellowship with a group of believers like this. You look around the room—each of those present seems to have an assignment from heaven. You wonder what God can do with a group like this.

What I have just described (with some artistic license) is a meeting of the Clapham Sect in the 1780s. The laughing Bill is William Wilberforce, best known for his tireless work in the abolishment of the British slave trade. He and others in the group cooperated to advance the gospel and push back darkness in London, Great Britain, and beyond. What can God do with a group like this? Well, history tells us that He can change the world forever!

The goal here is not to gaze longingly into the past. Why look backward other than to see that there is a historical Kingdom precedent for groups of believers who know their calling to turn the world upside down?

What if groups of believers with a clear sense of their heavenly assignments were the norm rather than the exception? What if pastors and Christian leaders like you and me were actively, intentionally, and consistently working to equip the Marys and Williams and Chucks in our congregations to carry the torches of revival and reformation into their Monday morning assignments?

Well, this is a book about how to do just that. Each chapter is written by a different author. This is a collection of voices that God is raising up in this time to teach the church how to activate every member for their calling in Christ.

The authors bring a diversity of rich insights from varying theological and workplace perspectives. Each has a significant background in conventional ministry or the marketplace, and often in both.

The authors didn't coordinate their contributions, so there is nuance and varying perspectives. But, overall, there is a harmony that I believe is born of the timeliness of what the Lord is speaking to the body of Christ in this hour.

It has been an honor and privilege to serve as a contributing author and the editor of this work.

—Jason Benedict

1
Blessings and Battles
David and Jason Benham

Our business careers started shortly after we got out of professional baseball. Neither of us had any formal training whatsoever—no classes, no books, nothing. We were history majors at Liberty University, which was basically a degree to work toward while waiting for the Major League draft.

But we were armed with the principles and stories of the Bible, passed down to us by our pastor dad. He taught us to love the Bible and apply it to every area of our lives. The more we applied its principles to our work, the more we realized that Scripture was a manual for business development.

With the Bible as our guide, we were able to develop our first business, Benham Real Estate, and a family of businesses that grew to multiple companies—both for-profit and non-profit—across the nation and in other parts of the world.

If you combine a disciplined work ethic with a commitment to do business God's way, then just buckle up and watch what happens. But please hear us: None of this will amount to anything if you gain it all and miss the mark—the divine purpose God has for your life and the people He's entrusted to your care.

We know how to build a business. We know how to make money. But we also know those things don't mean squat if you have to forfeit key relationships to make it happen.

It means nothing to land a million-dollar deal if your daughter won't talk to you. What does it matter if your company is worth half a billion when divorce papers are sitting on your desk? Who the heck cares that you own a private jet if you're walking away from God's will?

This was the beauty of building our business on the principles of the Bible; it continually reminded us of what true success was. It wasn't defined in terms of money or accolades or opening new locations. It was defined by thriving relationships—with God and people—and impacting those relationships for His glory.

> It means nothing to land a million-dollar deal if your daughter won't talk to you.

You see, the question is not, "How good is my business?" or, "How much money do I make?" The question is, "How deep are my relationships, and how can I use my business to bless the other people in them?"

The Bible is a book about relationships—between God and the people He created. He blesses us so we can bless others; and if you can master relationships, you can excel in business.

Every new business we open gets the same message:

- Our core is relationships.
- Our foundation is the Bible.
- Our goal is LIFE.

We want to breathe life into communities around the globe through the avenue of business based upon biblical principles.

But here's a crucial fact: The Bible isn't just a guide for relationships at home and a manual for success at work. It's also a weapon for battle against the devil and his schemes. When you apply God's Word to your life, you'll find that not only does success chase you down ... so does trouble.

We discovered this in the spring of 2014 after we signed a deal with HGTV to do a reality show on our business. Shortly after we started filming, and as commercials on our show began to run, liberal activists demanded the network pull the plug. They didn't like how vocal we were about faith in God and His design for marriage and the unborn.

Long before HGTV came our way, we felt God wanted us to use our voices to speak out about the moral evil taking place in our culture. Specifically, we knew God wanted us to do something about the plight of the unborn and say something about the redefinition of marriage. Plenty of other businesses pumped millions of dollars into Planned Parenthood and voiced their support for the redefinition of marriage, so we decided to do the same—just on the other side (the unpopular side).

We admit that doing this was much easier before we had experienced any success. Yet with a thriving national brand and a reality show on the line, the ballgame changed. If we spoke up, we'd better make sure to buckle up—because it could cost us something.

And cost us, it did. The pressure from the activist groups was so extreme that a few months before our show was set to air, HGTV fired us.

We found ourselves living out a great dichotomy: Applying the truths of the Bible to our work brought us promotion, but applying them to our walk brought us persecution. The same principles that got us hired got us fired. However, the Lord used even this to propel us into our ministry.

> "Who told you that you weren't in full-time ministry?"

Full-Time Ministry

Following God's lead, our real estate franchise exploded. And each year, our franchisees would fly in for our annual conference where we'd train them in Kingdom business, eat good BBQ, and hit group workouts where some—not all—even threw up (true story). At one of these conferences, God spoke something to us that changed our lives forever.

I (Jason) was speaking to our group about the true definition of profit, and about halfway through my talk, I heard God speak to me. I was a little caught off-guard because I don't typically hear voices in my head (that's David's thing). But that morning, I felt like I heard God whisper a question in my spirit.

"Who told you that you weren't in full-time ministry?"

That question may sound odd to you, but for me it rocked me to my core. It affected David the same way when I told him about it later that day.

You see, ever since we started our business, we struggled with guilt for not going into "full-time ministry."

We had no idea that our entire paradigm of ministry was off. We even started thinking that maybe our role was to make money so we could fund ministries, but that paradigm was just as broken.

What we didn't realize then, but we know now, is that we were in ministry the whole time. We learned that where we're placed and how we're paid doesn't determine the minister. It's about God's presence in our lives—and our passion to glorify Him through our work—that makes us full-time ministers right where we are.

It doesn't matter what we did for a living—ministry is about desire more than your duty. We had a desire to glorify God in our work, and that's what made us ministers.

This is a breakthrough paradigm shift Satan doesn't want you to have. He knows that how you see yourself determines how you behave yourself. So, if you see yourself as just an insurance agent, or banker, or contractor, or teacher, then that's how you'll behave. You won't act like the minister God made you to be.

Business is all about serving people. When you do it with a heart to please God, you've now turned your business into a ministry. It's more than just business *as* mission; its business *is* mission. You will see your business not just having instrumental value where you can use it to give money, but you will see it having intrinsic value where you can use it to do ministry.

God asked Adam a similar question after he sinned in the Garden and hid himself because he realized, for the first time, he was naked. God asked him, "Who told you that you were naked?" (Genesis 3:11 NLT) God had to deal with the liar in Adam's ear before He could set him straight.

We had been lied to for the first six years of our business. We believed that the only ministers were the people who stood onstage and spoke and operated through a nonprofit model—and that the only missionaries were the ones who went overseas and raised financial support.

But these were lies Satan wanted Jeff Van Duzer (author of *Why Business Matters to God*) to believe because he knew that if we saw our true identity as ministers on mission to represent God's Kingdom to earth, then he'd have a fight on his hands.

> How you see determines how you act.

Billy Graham once said, "I believe the next great move of God will be among believers in the marketplace." We believe this, too, and it starts when Christians in the workplace recognize their identities as ministers and their calling as missionaries.

God's question that day changed the trajectory of our lives. We no longer thought about getting out of business so we could enter into ministry. We thought about opening more businesses so we could do more ministry. Nothing in our circumstances had changed, but everything was different.

We had a new lens, and most believers in business need a new lens through which they can view themselves and their businesses.

How you see determines how you act. When perception changes, behavior changes. The single best thing we've ever done in our business is change the way we view it.

We have seen firsthand the power of this shift in perspective. If we can get an entrepreneur to see differently, his behavior will change naturally. And when this happens, buckle up and get ready for the ride because it's going to be a wild one.

Your True Identity

When we coach entrepreneurs, we always take them through the process in this order—paradigms, principles, practicals. Building your business on foundational principles is key, but all good principles are first derived from a proper paradigm.

> You're a minister right where you are.

God took the scales off our eyes that morning and showed us three paradigm-shifting truths that we now teach Christian entrepreneurs all over the world:

- You're a minister right where you are.
- You're on mission to bring God glory.
- Your work is worship.

If you don't get anything else out of this chapter other than these three truths, we will have accomplished our goal. When you know these truths and live them every day in your job or at your business, watch how God will show up and bless your socks off.

You may not be blessed with financial profit, but you will certainly be blessed with spiritual peace. Best of all, you will become the person God created you to be—someone who will not gain the world and forfeit his soul.

From our paradigm-shifting moment forward, everything changed for us. Our daily tasks turned into assignments from God. The people we worked with became a flock to be shepherded. Those we worked for turned into a mission field to be harvested.

We no longer operated out of guilt for not going into ministry, but out of gratitude for being in ministry. Our sense of failure was replaced with fulfillment as we realized we were right where God wanted us, using the talents He had given us, to be good at that in which He called us.

As a result of our newfound identities as ministers in the marketplace, we pressed the gas on our entrepreneurial drives and let them fly. Soon, we found ourselves atop a family of companies—both for profit and nonprofit—across the nation and around the globe.

Missioneering

Our success in business afforded us the opportunity to start several new initiatives, both in the for-profit and nonprofit space. We want to mention one initiative, in particular, that would be of interest to you as an entrepreneur (pastor).

In 2010, in the middle of the economic and housing crisis, we heard a statistic that 600 missionary families per month were leaving the mission field because Western funding had dried up. The problem wasn't a lack of missionaries; the problem was the lack of financial sustainability to keep them on the field.

We wondered what we could do about this disparity. Then it hit us; after much prayer, that we could do the same thing we had done time and time again in business—look in our bag to see what we had to offer. Like the young boy whose lunch Jesus used to feed the 5,000, we just offered what we had.

As entrepreneurs who created systems and rallied people toward a common vision, we could create a sustainable business to solve this problem of insufficient funding. Everything we had learned as entrepreneurs equipped us in the area of financial sustainability. This is what we had in our bag.

The light bulb went off in our heads. We had an idea! We could start a business overseas to meet tangible needs, hire local people, and give missionaries a place to work and minister while getting paid.

We called it Missioneering.

It would be a strategic attempt to bring together entrepreneurial business endeavors and Christian missionary work. Missioneering would be a combination of pioneering and engineering, with a heart for missions. It would require us to abandon the "two-sphere" mindset that there is a sacred secular division between vocation and ministry.

God had already been teaching us about this. The more we read the Bible, the more we grew convinced that faith can (and should) be practiced in the midst of the workplace. We learned that we were ministers right where we were, in our place of work. And our business was our ministry.

Our own company had proven to be a prototype for this paradigm, and now we had the desire to replicate it overseas to accomplish the same objective.

So that's what we did. And it worked!

The result was a self-sustaining revenue engine that could train and fund indigenous nationals who could reach their own culture and beyond for Christ. Our idea did not replace traditional missions, but simply strengthened it for God's glory.

Our first missioneering company was created in 2010. We started it as an outsourcing business based in the Philippines. Basically, the company handles any business processes that require a phone or computer; we have a large staff of trained professionals to accomplish those tasks.

> It is no wonder the Apostle Paul's tent business was a mission for him!

Our first objective was to bring real value to the city by creating jobs through a Kingdom-minded business. We've employed literally thousands of Filipinos who are truly grateful for the work.

On our last trip to the Philippines, we received roaring applause from our employees because they were all so thankful for steady employment. It was humbling. As of early 2021, we have over 1,500 employees there.

Our second objective was to disciple our employees at work, as well as their families at home. In our first year of business, we had seventy employees come to know the Lord. Our pastoral missioner, who is a paid member of our staff, discipled them. These numbers have grown tremendously through the years.

Our third objective was to engage the spiritual leaders of the city. At one point we had over 150 pastors and spiritual leaders meeting for monthly prayer, where they are encouraged and equipped by our missioneers.

Our final objective was to use our company profits to support indigenous missionaries to reach the unreached and unengaged. All the profits stay in the Philippines and are recirculated toward these objectives, as well as used to start new missioneering businesses. From the fruit of that first business, we were able to start several other businesses in the area.

So, how did we start?

First, we found a missionary already on the field who had the same heart to bring tangible value to his city through work. His name was Kevin Cracknell, and he had been in the Philippines for seven years. But his financial support was dwindling, along with his ability to influence the governing authorities of the city. He knew something needed to change.

We shared with him our concept—and it was the spark he was looking for. We funded the venture and then put him on our payroll with the task of finding a staff and location. He was all over it, and he knocked that task out of the park.

While he was working on all this, the four of us were back in the States drumming up business to send his way. We landed a couple of contracts, taught him how to deliver the service according to the clients' requirements, and he and his team of Filipinos accomplished the work. A few months later and forty employees deep, we realized we were on to something.

Early on, we knew that only one missioneer wouldn't be enough if we wanted to grow. So, God brought us two more missioneers who held strategic positions in the company. Trent Pruett served as our minister to the people (pastoral missioneer) while Ajit Sivarajan served as our minister to the process (process missioneer).

Our pastoral missioneer was responsible for:
- Shepherding the hearts of the people
- Organizing discipleship

- Developing community
- Helping with human resources

Our process missioneer was responsible for:

- Business excellence
- Quality control
- Client retention
- Customer service

Our pastoral and process missioneers worked together as engineers (business and personnel infrastructure), while our original missioneer (Kevin) acted more as a pioneer (finding and starting new businesses). Although our missioneers had different roles and responsibilities—with a lot of overlap—all of them were on mission to see God's Kingdom advance in their city. We've watched these three work together with incredible Christian unity that has yielded supernatural results.

With over 1,500 employees—many of whom have received Christ—we are also servicing dozens of clients from all over the world. And it has been inspiring to see the incredible favor we've received with the leaders of the city because of the amount of revenue and jobs we have generated.

In addition, through the profits and influence of our company, our missioneers have started a sports league, evangelism outreaches, disaster relief projects, monthly Bible studies, an orphanage, and now a budding church. Support for these programs comes from simply creating value in the marketplace.

The amazing thing is how much direct evangelism and discipleship ends up taking place when a business is owned and run by Christians who see themselves as ministers of God. Our team has an unbelievable amount of consistent contact with people on a daily basis.

It is no wonder the Apostle Paul's tent business was a mission for him! He was right where everyone else was, in the marketplace. He got paid to meet their physical needs while simultaneously meeting their spiritual needs. Having two hours of a congregation's time on a Sunday morning is good, but having forty hours of their time Monday through Friday takes discipling to a whole new level.

> Vocation and mission don't have to be split apart in a false division.

Just as our first missioneering business was beginning to take off, two of our missioneers found additional business opportunities in the city as well. Kevin and Trent came to us with a concept we all loved. They wanted to open fitness facilities in the busiest parts of town.

Boom! Now that was right up our alley.

What's great is that we were able to use the profit from our first missioneering company to fund these additional missioneering projects. We opened two CrossFit gyms in 2012. Our trainers taught gym members that "physical training is of some value, but Godliness has value for all things" (1 Timothy 4:8 NIV). And they got paid to teach this! Our CrossFit gyms were simply tools to bring the Gospel of God's Kingdom right into the busiest parts of the city.

As a result of the increased popularity of our gyms, our missioneers gained the respect of local media and government officials as well. Interestingly, many high-ranking officials and well-known media became members.

It was fun to watch our missioneers and their wives receive invitations to holiday parties with cultural and political leaders. One of our guys was actually featured on the cover of the city's largest magazine and in the local news.

But that's not the best part. We were then able to sell those gyms and use the funds to purchase a piece of land that now houses an orphanage for abandoned kids.

In the Bible, blessings are both spiritual and economic (Genesis 12:2–3). This is not a "prosperity" message, but simply a truth that Christians can lead the way by being a blessing to other people. And one of the best ways to do this is through the avenue of work. Vocation and mission don't have to be split apart in a false division. God never intended this.

Missioneering was our attempt to create something that in the long term was both economically sustainable and beneficial to the Kingdom. We would absolutely love it if entrepreneurs around the world would read this and say, "Hey, I can do something like that. I've always seen myself only as a businessperson, but now I realize that I'm also a minister of the Gospel right where I am, and my business is a ministry to extend God's Kingdom."

You don't have to go overseas to be a missioneer. A good friend of ours, JD Gibbs—son of Hall of Fame football coach Joe Gibbs—asked us to meet him for lunch one day to discuss what he could do to impact his city for the Lord. He wanted to provide money to a ministry that was close to his heart, but he wanted to do more than just give money; he wanted to create a stream of sustainability.

When we outlined the concept of missioneering to him, JD was hooked. We suggested that he take the money he wanted to donate and convert it into a wealth-generating river, which could be done by investing in a business and naming the ministry as the beneficiary.

In this way, he would create a dual ministry—the business itself (the employees and patrons of the business) and the funds for the other ministry. The ministry is called Safe Haven and is run by Trent and his wife, Amy.

And you know what? He did it. He opened a sandwich shop and used the funds to support that ministry.

Today, JD has gone home to be with the Lord. He was an amazing husband and father, and his legacy of stewarding God's resources (his talent and money) to expand God's Kingdom live on to this day in our hometown of Charlotte, North Carolina.

This is how Christians can live powerfully in the world. We must see ourselves as ministers of God, seamlessly weaving vocation and mission together. These were never to be separated in the first place. We have to abandon the old paradigm of the sacred/secular divide and get back to the reality that everything God has made is sacred, which includes our work.

As Kingdom entrepreneurs:

- Our destination is God's Kingdom.
- Our vehicle is God's work.
- Our fuel is God's love.

There's no stopping that combo!

Questions for Reflection and Application

1. The brothers talk about how their pastor dad taught them to apply the principles of the Bible to every area of life, and they attribute their success and kingdom impact to doing life and business this way. Many pastors would agree with this concept of whole life application of the Bible—why is it that, by and large, we don't see the average church member applying biblical principles to their work life the way the brothers do?

2. The brothers have a revelation of their work life as full-time ministry. They call this a breakthrough paradigm shift. What could you do to help others understand this truth?

3. David and Jason coin the term *missioneering* to describe pioneering businesses with very intentional integration of vocation and ministry. They describe their experience in building these self-sustaining revenue engines. Brainstorm ways that a similar approach could bless your community.

Twin brothers David and Jason Benham are former professional baseball players, nationally acclaimed entrepreneurs, and bestselling authors. Their first company grew to 100 offices in 35 states and catapulted them onto the national stage. Their commitment to "building business God's way" allowed them to top charts like *Inc.* magazine's fastest-growing companies, Franchise 500's top new franchises, and Ernst & Young Entrepreneurs of the Year finalists.

After building an international company with more than 1,000 employees and hosting an HGTV reality show, the brothers built a thriving community of faith-filled entrepreneurs, called Expert Ownership, to equip and empower believers to stand strong for the faith in the midst of a morally declining culture.

2
Loving Monday as Much as You Already Love Sunday

Dr. Ed Silvoso

What happens in church every Sunday is indeed extraordinary. The Word is preached, people worship God, and there is repentance, reconciliation, and much more, all of which is spiritually invigorating. Nothing comes a close second to that. But what must be done so that what happens once a week will happen every day in the marketplace?

Sunday is the highlight of the week for believers, but what about Monday? We usually don't wake up on Mondays with a smile, but Jesus is the same yesterday, today, and forever. This means that He is the Lord of Monday and every other weekday as much as He is Lord of Sunday. How can we experience that?

First, we need to determine at what level we find ourselves in the marketplace. I wish to suggest that there are four levels of involvement for believers in the marketplace. Level one is not a good one: Christians who *barely survive in the marketplace.*

The next level up is Christians who *apply biblical principles,* but they do it for the marketplace not to change them, instead of them changing the marketplace. The third level is Christians who *operate in the power of the Holy Spirit in the marketplace.* They don't just go to work; they go to minister in the workplace.

A case study that I describe in detail in my book *Ekklesia: Rediscovering God's Instrument for Global Transformation* is the story of Wanlapa. Because she was unemployed, her pastor bought her a motorized tricycle to sell ice cream in Phuket, Thailand. After reading *Anointed for Business*, she realized, "I am a minister in the marketplace and this tricycle is like a chariot of fire."

> Yes, it is possible to operate in the marketplace in the power of the Holy Spirit!

She proceeded to anoint it, dedicate the ice cream to the Lord, and then pray for her clients as they approached her. As people ate the ice cream, a surprising number felt a touch from God. Why? Why not? It's biblical. In Acts 19:11, Paul's garments delivered people oppressed by demons and healed the sick. Furthermore, if Peter's shadow healed people, why not merchandise dedicated to God *à la* Acts 19:10–11?

So much happened around that ice cream cart that she was able to lead close to 700 people to the Lord. Emboldened by this, she set her evangelistic sights on the governor. Every day she stopped by his residence, but she knew she could never go inside because she was socially insignificant. Instead, she sent him blessings *à la* Luke 10 (prayer evangelism).

Eventually, the governor came out, bought an ice cream, and had a power encounter! Seeing this, she invited him to church. Miraculously, he went, got saved, and dedicated the government to God. Yes, it is possible to operate in the marketplace in the power of the Holy Spirit! But as exciting as this third level is, it is not the final destination. There is more!

The next level up is Christians who operate in the power of the Holy Spirit *to transform the marketplace*. In that context, I want to share about Michael Brown, a believer with a thriving, profitable school bus transportation company, Michael's Transportation. After he heard the teaching from *Anointed for Business*, he realized, "I am not just a businessman; I am a minister in the marketplace."

Brown anointed every bus as a "mobile ark of the covenant." He invited God the Father to be the chairman of the board, Jesus the CEO, and the Holy Spirit the legal counsel. Under their guidance, he provided resources for struggling schools and trained felons released from prison as professional drivers.

The spiritual climate changed, first in his company and then in the city. The company that had a revenue of $2 million per year before he dedicated it to God has now surpassed $20 million. To address the problem of systemic poverty, he sold shares in the company to his employees and together they are transforming an entire county in Northern California.

Is it possible to transform the marketplace? Yes, but the deeper issue is how and why to do it. For that, we need to understand that the marketplace is the combination of business, education, and government. That trio constitutes the heart of the city. To change a person, his or her heart has to be changed; to change a city, its marketplace has to be transformed.

We know it is possible to change the marketplace because politicians do it all the time when they change laws. As a result, the city, state, or the nation changes. But the question that occupies us today is: Is it biblical? And the answer is a resounding *yes!* The key is found in Luke 19:10, and it's the word *that*:

> "For the Son of Man [Jesus Christ] has come to seek and save [not just the lost] *that* which was lost" (emphasis added).

What is it that was lost when sin entered creation? First, our relationship with God. Adam and Eve were cast out of His presence. Second, our relationship with each other. Adam and Eve no longer got along, Cain murdered Abel, and so forth from that moment on.

But the third thing that Jesus came to recover was the marketplace because when the ground was cursed, what before was given freely and plentifully, now had to be earned with the sweat of man's brow. Jesus came to seek and to save everything that was lost, which includes your company, your school, and the government.

This is further confirmed by Colossians 1:19–20: "For it was the Father's good pleasure [He enjoyed doing it] to reconcile all things to himself."

Where are those things? Whether they are on earth, or in heaven, they are reconciled. That means they are redeemed. We see this clearly spelled out in Ephesians 1:7–10: "In Him [in Jesus] we have redemption through His blood, according to the riches of His grace, that He might gather together [not only souls] all things in Christ, both in heaven and on earth."

If I say coffee, bacon, and eggs, what would you say by word association? Breakfast, right? If I say, as the verse reads, redemption, blood, and grace, what comes to mind? The Cross and the salvation emanating from it. Receive the truth that the same blood that saved you has also redeemed every institution where you are serving, working, or overseeing!

This becomes even more clear when we consider the context for Luke 19:10. It shows the salvation of a marketplace influencer, Zacchaeus. He was not a saint; in fact, he was a traitor to his nation by working for the Romans as a tax collector, which required not only a great deal of social insensitivity, but especially greed.

It is no wonder that his neighbors were amazed when he took half of the money and gave it to the poor, and then set the other half aside to make up for wrongs he had committed. Such radical actions reveal not only his personal salvation, but also that of his household.

This is a very important term because *house* in the Bible consists of people, their family, and also their workplace, as most people in biblical times worked out of the home. The same salvation that came to you must also come to your workplace to be reclaimed the way that Zacchaeus' was.

Starting in Luke 19:11, Jesus goes on to tell the parable of the minas because He was nearing Jerusalem. He wanted to show that the Kingdom must come to every city before it came to Jerusalem.

A mina was a unit of money and in this story, the master told his disciples to go and do business, obviously in the marketplace. While he was away, his enemies took over the marketplace, but his servants continued to do business. Upon his return, he asked, "How well did you do?"

Based on their replies, he continued, "Because I gave you one and you got ten," or, "I gave you one, and you got five, I'm giving you authority to oversee cities!"

Likewise, today the Lord wants you to do business successfully, even in a hostile environment, for you to become head and not tail, to be above and not below, not only for your own pleasure, but to take the Kingdom of God where the Gates of Hades are, so that eventually you will reclaim your company the way Michael Brown has done.

Why is this important? Because it highlights the three-dimensional nature of Jesus's redemptive work. First, it's personal; He saved people. Second, it's interpersonal; He restored relationships. And third, it redeemed the marketplace. Now, it still must be reclaimed the way you and I were reclaimed (we were saved 2,000 years ago), but somebody brought the Gospel to us, and we got reclaimed.

> Actually, we don't *go* to church. *We are the church.*

It's very important to put this in a broader context. There is definitely a call to the pulpit, but if all believers are priests (that is, ministers), then there should be an equally divine call to the marketplace. The priesthood of all believers has two dimensions—vertical and horizontal.

Pastors understand the vertical better than anyone, and believers in the marketplace understand the horizontal quite well. We must bring both dimensions together because when they are integrated, extraordinary things happen all week long, and not just on Sundays.

To better capture this truth, we must realize that many wrongly think that we *go to church,* but actually, we don't *go* to church, *we are the church.*

What does it mean to be the church? To find the answer, we must address some very intriguing questions that spawned my book *Ekklesia.* If the church is so important (and it is), why did Jesus speak only twice about it in the Gospels?

Furthermore, why is it that there are no instructions or a command on church planting in the New Testament, as important as church planting is? We know the Apostles definitely planted churches. How does the church today compare?

Let's look at the metrics of the ekklesia in the New Testament. Number one, members were devoted to their leaders' teaching. Number two, they enjoyed personal and corporate prosperity to meet the needs inside and outside of their circles. Number three, there was daily numerical growth. Number four, they had ongoing and expanding favor with outsiders. And number five, signs and wonders were a recurring phenomenon.

It was clearly a different kind of church, or at least it looked different than what we see today. It was always people, never buildings. It was vibrant, expansive, operating 24/7, with an unstoppable capacity for growth. It set the agenda rather than being an item on somebody else's agenda.

So, the obvious question is, why such low performance and little social relevance today? Could it be that we have confined to four walls once a week, what is meant to operate 24/7 all over the city?

The other side of the church is the Kingdom of God. They are two sides of the same coin and, as such, they go together. When Jesus launched the church, He described the Kingdom as leaven, light, water, and salt.

Leaven in a jar doesn't do what it's supposed to do. Light that is blocked creates darkness. Water that doesn't run becomes putrid. Salt in a shaker doesn't do any good to the meal. We need to take these into society. Is there something that we haven't tapped into yet? And if so, what is it?

There were three main institutions in Israel during New Testament days: the temple, the synagogue, and the church, the Ekklesia, which is the word translated *church* in our Bibles. The temple was a religious place where people met with representatives of God, the priests. The synagogue was another religious place where God's people met with each other.

But the ekklesia, the secular ekklesia, was a Roman institution. It was an assembly of people deputized by the Emperor to introduce and implement the laws of the empire. The function of that ekklesia was to teach the language and culture of Rome. Because the concept of the secular ekklesia was part of everyday life in Israel, Jesus did not have to elaborate on it, except to describe His Ekklesia vis-à-vis its secular counterpart.

Very interestingly, Jesus didn't say, "I will build My temple," or, "I will build My synagogue," but He stated, "I shall build *My* Ekklesia." Basically, He was implying that a secular ekklesia already exists and it's governed by evil forces described as the Gates of Hades. But He will release a new Ekklesia, a group of people (because Ekklesia means an assembly of people) and when the two meet, His will win.

Let's pay attention to Jesus's strategy. He co-opted a major institution that was operating in the marketplace with imperial authority and infused it with God's Kingdom DNA. He went beyond that by also co-opting the conventus. A conventus came into being when two or more Roman citizens came together, an action that resulted in the power and authority of the emperor being with them.

Isn't that what Jesus said about His church? When two or three of His disciples get together, He will be there in their midst, granting them power to bind and to release in His name? In addition, He co-opted the term *apostle*.

Today it's a religious term, but in Jesus's day it was used to describe the admiral in charge of a fleet loaded with building materials and artisans with building expertise (carpenters, plumbers, engineers, architects) sent out to build a city that looked like Rome in a new territory.

Consider this: Jesus co-opted the Ekklesia, He co-opted the conventus, and He also co-opted the office of apostle. That's why, when you are commissioned as a minister in the marketplace, you are one of those ships taking building materials to establish the Kingdom of God in new territory.

In the Bible, the Ekklesia was a building-less mobile people movement, designed to operate 24/7 in the marketplace to impact everybody and everything. By selecting the Ekklesia model over the temple or the synagogue, Jesus chose an agency better suited to succeed in the marketplace because His ultimate objective was to see nations discipled by inserting the leaven of His Kingdom into their social fiber through the Ekklesia, which is people.

Jesus's Ekklesia is not meant to be a sterile, sanitized holding tank in which His disciples were to store in frozen isolation converts fished out of a turbulent and doomed sea to await the arrival of the refrigerator ship that would transfer them to a heavenly port for final processing.

No! Instead, His Ekklesia—whether in the embryonic expression of the conventus or in a more expansive version—was designed to inject the leaven of the Kingdom of God into the dough of society, so that first people, and then cities, and eventually nations would be discipled.

We can take inspiration from the Apostle Paul. In Acts 19:10–11 (LEB), we read, "All who lived in Asia heard the word of the Lord ... And God was performing extraordinary miracles by the hands of Paul."

Who performed the miracles? God. Whose hands did He use? Paul's. Where is God? He's here. Where is Paul? He's not here. Who is here today? You. God wants to use you to perform extraordinary miracles. How did they work? It says in the Bible that handkerchiefs or aprons were carried from Paul's body to the sick.

He was working making tents, and the diseases left them, and the evil spirits went out. Why? Because Paul was a minister in the marketplace, and whatever came in touch with him in the workplace became a vehicle for transformation. Today, whatever you do and touch is potentially a vehicle for transformation!

The place where you work is where you spend the bulk of your time every week. When you take the leaven of the Kingdom there, you begin to reclaim it for God, and you can become another Michael Brown or Wanlapa.

The key is to realize that you are the Ekklesia, and when you get together with another believer, you obtain quorum to invite the presence of Jesus ... and when He shows up, He performs miracles. This is the anointing I pray these scriptural truths will lead you to receive!

Now, let me share a word of caution. In the Bible, we find two characters that we greatly appreciate because of their service to God: Moses and Solomon. Both were given similar assignments, to build a place where God would dwell. In Moses's case, the task involved the tent of the tabernacle and the Ark of the Covenant, where the presence of God was. In Solomon's case, it was building the temple.

Both received extraordinary and unique assignments. Both completed them. But when Moses was done, he had grown stronger in his walk with God, whereas Solomon had lost his fervor. He became distracted by pagan wives, and he committed sins he shouldn't have committed.

> The Lord should be the owner of the company instead of you.

How can one person finish such an amazing job and be stronger, and the other fail? Because Moses relied on divine revelation. Bezalel (who was his number-two guy) is the first person in the Bible we are told was filled with the Holy Spirit for the blueprint that was in heaven to be replicated on Earth.

Do you know that there is a blueprint in heaven for your destiny? Yes, God's destiny for you in your life, in your family, in your neighborhood, and in the workplace. And for this to happen, you have to be filled with the Holy Spirit like Bezalel was.

I like to imagine that Solomon, on the other hand, Googled "best secular practices" and "best temple builders." Who came up in the search results? Hiram, king of Lebanon. Solomon must have said, "Hey, would you help me build this?" And he did, but in the process, this became a channel for idolatry that led Solomon astray.

Like Moses and Solomon, you stand at a fork in the road. You can be a minister that operates in the fullness of the Holy Spirit, or you can end up like Solomon, doing God's work using best secular practices instead of divine anointing, and growing weaker in the process.

I want to plant a seed for your prayerful consideration. Having a "Kingdom company" is great, compared to the days when Kingdom companies were unknown. But to really enjoy the fullness of God in your life and in the marketplace, you must envision a *King's* company.

The Lord should be the owner of the company instead of you. It could be a very humble ice cream cart like Wanlapa, or a prosperous multimillion-dollar company like Michael's Transportation ... it shouldn't be *your* company, but *the King's* company. And that's why I encourage you—in fact, I challenge you—dedicate yourself and dedicate your company to the Lord, be trained, and live up to the fullness of your divine destiny!

In conclusion, let the Holy Spirit speak to you. Let Him impress on you the tremendous faith that God has in you because He is saying, "You will rebuild the ancient ruins, you will raise up the age-old foundation, you will repair the breach" (Isaiah 58). And you will be called, like Michael Brown and Wanlapa, "restorers of the streets in which to live."

Pray this prayer: Holy Spirit, I pray that You overpower me the way You overpowered the Virgin Mary when she asked, "How can I do that? I'm a virgin!"

The Holy Spirit will come upon you as He came upon Mary to deposit a divine seed. Let Him baptize you right now. In the name of Jesus. He's doing it. Feel His presence; feel His power.

The insights that I have shared, the documentation that is available, can make you pregnant, so that when you go to work on Monday and every day afterward, you will love it as much as you love Sunday because you will be a minister in the marketplace empowered to change the world!

Questions for Reflection and Application

1. What are some practical ways you can challenge believers in the marketplace to move from mere marketplace survival to walking in the power of the Holy Spirit to transform the marketplace?

2. Dr. Silvoso describes the historical, contextual meanings of the words *ekklesia, conventus,* and *apostle*. How can our definitions impact our effectiveness? Do you need a biblical upgrade in any of your definitions?

Dr. Ed Silvoso, founder and president of Harvest Evangelism and the leader of the Transform Our World Network, is a strategist and Bible teacher who specializes in nation and marketplace transformation. Trained in both theology and business, he is the author of numerous books, including the bestselling *Anointed for Business* and *Ekklesia.*

His work experience includes banking, hospital administration, financial services, and church ministry, as well as coaching leaders on how to take the power and presence of God into the marketplace to see their sphere of influence transformed.

Dr. Silvoso and his wife, Ruth, have four married daughters and twelve grandchildren.

www.transformourworld.org
www.edsilvoso.com

3
Spiritual Covering and the Symbiotic Relationship Between the Local Church and Businesspeople

David Hodgson

If there is one thing which I would implore all pastors to consider when building relationships with the businesspeople in their congregations, it is the provision of a strong and active spiritual covering. This is, by far, the best answer to that ubiquitous statement so often uttered by businesspeople: "The pastor is not interested in me; he or she just wants my money."

As the leader of Kingdom Investors (KI), one of the largest and most influential marketplace ministries in the world, and as the owner and managing director of a billion-dollar corporation comprising over thirty companies, I very often come across the tension between the "Kings and the Priests."

At almost every venue where I have lectured over the last eighteen years, I have been approached by disillusioned businesspeople who have left the local church because of conflict or disagreement between themselves and the church leadership.

At KI, we certainly attract a lot of businesspeople who have left church and are looking for an alternative. KI is definitely not a church, nor is it a substitute for the local church, as it operates on a different "mountain of influence" under a different mandate than the church, but disgruntled businesspeople flock to us regardless.

In the title of this chapter, I deliberately included the word "symbiotic" to describe the relationship between the local church and the businesspeople simply because neither one can survive without the other! Of course, the correct meaning of symbiotic is "mutually beneficial."

However, I am using it in a stronger context because I know I would have been taken out completely by the devil if I did not have the spiritual covering provided to me by my local church. And I also know my church would not have survived financially if it had not provided this covering to me and to others.

I know this because I was sent to this church in 2000 to help rebuild it financially. I have been on the church board for eighteen years; I see the figures, and I know where the funds come from.

In Australia, 10% of the population owns a business. This ratio is reflected in our church. When our church conducts its Miracle Offering appeal each year to fund its vision for the next twelve months, the offerings from 90% of the church congregation are more than doubled by the 10% who own businesses.

I have lectured at hundreds of churches over the last two decades, and I know from discussions with pastors that this is not the norm. What I am saying is because our church has nurtured its businesspeople properly, it is financially very strong and is always able to pay its expenses and fund its expansion.

And in return, we the businesspeople get this amazing spiritual "bulletproofing," which enables us to operate so much better in the marketplace than those who do not have it.

Over the rest of this chapter, I will explain what a spiritual covering actually is, why we need one, and then I will demonstrate it from the scriptures. I will punctuate it with snippets of what I teach wayward businesspeople when I come across them.

> The church itself is much bigger than we businesspeople are as individuals.

Thereafter, I will put it into a military context by describing a live operation during my time in the Special Forces whereby we were badly mauled by the enemy because we neglected our "covering." And finally, I will consolidate all of this into modern-day marketplace testimonies to prove the concept.

So, What Is Spiritual Covering?

Covering from the local church is a layer of protection that is afforded to the recipient by the institution of the church, which is conveyed through prayer, intercession, prophecy, meetings, and dialogue with the recipient—in this case, the businessperson.

The church itself is much bigger than we businesspeople are as individuals. It consists of hundreds of people, or thousands of people, or in some bigger churches, tens of thousands of people all in agreement and, to a large extent, of one accord.

If the church belongs to a denomination or a larger movement, then the covering is even more institutionalised and is backed up by a hierarchy of leadership, experience, and wisdom.

As an example, at the local level there are prayer meetings at our church, and the prayer leaders are intentionally instructed by the pastor to pray for every business by name on an ongoing basis. They do this corporately with the backing of the institution of the church.

Further to this, the pastor and church intercessors are praying for us and telling us what they hear. My pastor often tells me what he hears. Some of these prayer warriors email me and tell me what they are praying for. Often, they pull me up at church and tell me they have been praying for me. In other words, they are interacting personally with us.

My previous pastor used to come into our boardroom and pray with us. He also used to come in and coach my head office staff once a month. He has since retired, and Pastor Paul took over. Pastor Paul often calls me and books in a coffee or lunch with me, to get a feel for what is going on in my world, in my ministry, and in my company. This way, he knows what to pray for and what direction to give me.

He also wants to get a feel for what is going on in my assignment and therefore wants to know what we are doing or teaching at Kingdom Investors. This amounts to an accountability line so he can make sure I am not teaching rubbish, or that I have not turned into some crazy person advocating insurrection against the Australian Taxation Office in the name of God!

Pastor Paul attends every KI meeting here on the Sunshine Coast so that he can watch what is going on, what is taught, and get a feel for its impact and direction. All of this so he can pray for us and intercede for us—and prophesy for us as needed.

Another real key to this is that the pastor has taken time to understand the businesspeople. On Sunday, he told the church that he understands the risks we carry, and he understands the leadership and influence we carry in the marketplace. He fully understands the importance of "kings"—Christian businessmen and women—and in his own words, he loves and cares for us.

> I announce my spiritual covering at every lecture everywhere in the world.

I don't mind if it is not the pastor who has coffee with me, as there are many businesses, and he is busy. Especially in larger churches, it would not be possible for the senior pastor to provide a personal meeting with everyone. Instead, it could be any of the church leaders, or the connect group leaders if they are approved by the pastors as mature enough and, of course, the church intercessors. It is still the same spiritual mantle of spiritual DNA coming down the line, and it offers the same protection.

I'm sure you remember how Moses's father-in-law, Jethro, himself a Midianite Priest, came and taught Moses how to delegate good men (and women, of course, in the modern era), "able men, such as fear God, men of truth, hating unjust gain," to help him share the workload of looking after the people in Exodus 18.

The point is that it must be a legitimate covering provided by a qualified person who themselves has an accountability line that means they are representative of the local church.

I announce my spiritual covering at every lecture everywhere in the world. This is because I want everyone in the room, seen and unseen, to know that I am not an easy target and there are "able men, such as fear God, men of truth, hating covetousness" who are protecting me!

Why Do Businesspeople Need This Covering?

Our own studies from KI surveys since 2004 show unequivocally that those people who have a legitimate and comprehensive spiritual covering do much better in the marketplace than those who do not.

Running a business without a spiritual covering is like planning a battle without any intelligence reports on the enemy, and then going into battle without an air force. We cannot know everything in the spirit ourselves, and we are very often led by our souls into dangerous territory. Third-party covering protects against this.

We know as Christian businesspeople that our battles are in the spirit, which then manifest into the physical. The problem is when we lose those battles in the physical, the knock-on effect can be enormous.

We can lose our businesses, we can lose investor money which can put investors into financial hardship, and we ourselves fall into financial hardship. This often leads to marriage breakdown, suicide, substance abuse, homelessness, and much more. And, of course, we would not be able to fund our local church.

As kings in the marketplace, trying to oppose Babylon and usher in God's Kingdom on our own has never worked throughout history, simply because Babylon is too big and too powerful for us to take on individually without the army of God. After all, what is a king without an army? *Doomed!* Simply put, we need spiritual protection because we are warring in the spirit.

> Around half of the businesspeople that I lecture to have left the local church.

Why Have So Many Businesspeople Abandoned the Local Church?

Around half of the businesspeople that I lecture to have left the local church. If they leave church, by default they lose that local church covering, and they tend to start losing their battles in business. I know this from empirical data.

Our surveys reveal they leave for many different reasons. Here are the most common we have come across:

- The pastor doesn't care about me; he just wants my money.
- I found church to be a bad business model because lots of money is pumped in and nothing changes in the city.
- My church never achieves its vision such as, "We are going to take the city," but instead the money is spent on buildings.
- I am told if I sow, I will reap, and yet most of us never reap.

- Or they gave an offering of $20 grand and two weeks later, the pastor still has not invited them to dinner.
- Some say they see the holiness on Sunday and the hypocrisy on Monday—and, of course, many of them are part of it on Monday.
- Or silly things like, the pastor did not come over and greet me today.
- Another very common one is they try to control the pastor, and this leads to conflict. Many pastors tell me they are shy of businesspeople and don't court them in their churches because the businesspeople try to control them.

Here is what I say to those who try to control the pastor: Guys, we need to clearly understand that our role is to control the culture in the marketplace, not to control the pastor. Unless you are specifically on the board of the church, you shouldn't even have time to get involved in church politics. You have enough work to do overcoming a prolific enemy so that you can multiply your business.

I explain to them that my son used to be the youth pastor at my church. My current senior pastor used to be a member of my son's youth group! Think about that. My son used to be my pastor's youth pastor! Now Pastor Paul is my senior pastor. But even so, I still regard him as the senior spiritual authority. I come under his pastoral authority, I support the church financially, and I don't try to control him.

He is young, but very wise and well-trained, and our church is very influential in our community because the Kings and Priests work together. We are all covered in the marketplace, and we are all prospering because we know we cannot do without each other.

So, for all the above reasons, many businesspeople leave, and they try other churches where they find the same issues. Eventually, they leave church altogether and do their own thing. But the funny thing is, most of these ones who don't go to church are not prospering very well.

> Most of the businesspeople who don't go to church are not prospering very well.

They are still good Christians trying to do God's will, but very quickly they lose ground. They get picked off by the enemy because they cannot see it coming, as nobody has "got their spiritual back."

This is the very important symbiotic relationship between the Kings and the Priests that I spoke about earlier. It is almost transactional—the church needs our money, and we need their spiritual protection to generate that money. It really is that simple.

Once the businesspeople get this, they can go to church and fund the vision of the church. As long as the church is not building brothels, they shouldn't care what the church does with the money.

I explain to my businesspeople that once they have sown funds into the custody of the local church, the church is now accountable for it—not us. And I explain if they do that, they will find it is much more relaxing at church. Their marketplace activities will be aligned with God's will, and they will have a hedge of protection around them.

Here is something else I drill into my business audiences: Your spiritual covering needs to be strong. Because your spiritual covering comes from your local church, you should use whatever gifting God has given you to strengthen your local church. Inevitably, you would have the gift of finances over your lives; therefore, you should strengthen the church with your finances.

- Singers seem to do it; they use their gift to sing in church quite willingly.
- Ministry leaders seem to do it; they use their gift of leadership to lead ministries and home groups quite willingly.
- Counselors seem to do it; they visit homes, they look after people in distress, and so on, quite willingly.
- Prophets seem to do it; they prophesy for the church.
- Chefs seem to do it; they work in the church kitchens and cafés and church functions using their gifts to support their spiritual covering.
- But businesspeople, who have the gift to create wealth, seem to have issues with using their gift to support their covering.

Here is how I explain this to them: This is because your allegiance is to the assets, and not the supplier of the assets, who is God. This is called Mammon, and Mammon is the single largest and most influential deity that you will encounter in the marketplace. Using your gift to create wealth to support your spiritual covering in your local church is the very best way to overcome Mammon!

It's not always because of Mammon. Sometimes they just don't understand covering, or their church does not provide this and, therefore, they see no reason to go the extra mile.

So, What Does This Look Like in the Bible?

During the great exodus from Egypt, the Israelites clashed with the Amalekites when they arrived at Rephidim. Amalek was a warrior king, and the Amalekites were very experienced in combat. They were nomadic.

Their strategy was to attack and escape. They were like guerrilla warfare experts. Amalek was the grandson of Esau, and you will remember that Isaac had prophesied over Esau, "You shall live by the sword."

No one had ever been successful against the Amalekites, and at one point they even overran Egypt and became pharaohs for a period of time.

So, here was this elite army of skilled assault troops ambushing the stragglers at the rear of the Hebrew migration. They were deliberately killing the women, children, and the elderly. This did not stop the momentum, so the Amalekites overtook the Hebrews and blocked their passage, confronting them head-on at Rephidim.

Exodus 17:9 (KJV) tells us:

> And Moses said unto Joshua, Choose us out men, and go out, fight with Amalek: to morrow I will stand on the top of the hill with the rod of God in mine hand.

This is mission impossible, in case you had not figured this out. A bunch of slaves to fight the most experienced warriors in the whole of the Near East! But they had "the Rod of God" on their side—and it was wielded by a competent, tried, tested, qualified, and ordained man of God.

> We all need the Rod of God in our businesses and our churches.

Let me explain the Rod of God, and the fact that the person holding it was qualified to wield its power.

This is the same rod that God had used to perform all the miracles leading up to the exodus from Egypt. It was known as "the walking stick with the power of God" (Exodus 4:20 ERV) and with it, the impossible was achieved over and over and over again.

We all need the Rod of God in our businesses and our churches if we are going to achieve the impossible!

Moses told Joshua, "This is your assignment, Joshua. You go choose some men and go and attack them." Imagine Joshua. He was to take on an elite army, and all he had was an army of slaves with picks and shovels, inexperienced and untrained for war.

However, Moses promised to *cover* Joshua, to provide spiritual covering as Joshua fought in the battleground. This is what he said: "Tomorrow I will stand on the top of the hill with the staff of God in my hand." (Exodus 17:9 ESV)

Joshua obeyed and did his assignment. And Moses was on top of the hill to offer the spiritual covering (Exodus 17:10–13 ESV):

> So Joshua did as Moses told him, and fought with Amalek, while Moses, Aaron, and Hur went up to the top of the hill. Whenever Moses held up his hand, Israel prevailed, and whenever he lowered his hand, Amalek prevailed. But Moses' hands grew weary, so they took a stone and put it under him, and he sat on it, while Aaron and Hur held up his hands, one on one side, and the other on the other side. So his hands were steady until the going down of the sun. And Joshua overwhelmed Amalek and his people with the sword.

Israel's army of slaves defeated the elite troops because of the covering. Not just because the covering was there, but also because the covering was strong. There are two things to consider here, and here is how I explain this to my business audiences:

1. It does not have to be your senior pastor who personally provides this covering. It can be his or her leadership team, as they carry the same mantle and authority and spiritual DNA as their leader. This is why the covering also consisted of Aaron and Hur. These were subordinate to Moses, but they still came under the authority of the Rod of God, which symbolised the power of God, and they still won the battle. This applies today in the bigger churches where the pastor could never get to everyone individually but can use his or her leaders at any level to provide the one-on-one covering that is needed.

2. And secondly, it means very clearly that your spiritual covering needs to be strong—and well-

funded. When the covering was physically weak, Joshua lost; when it was strong, Joshua won. This should be very clear to all of us. We should be using our gifts to strengthen our spiritual covering. In other words, if you have the gift of finance, use it to fund your church so that your church is strong, and so that your church does not have to fret and worry and pray about where it will get money from—rather, have it praying for you!

And I am not just talking about funding the expenses of the church; I am talking about funding the *vision* of your church. If we really want to prosper in the marketplace, we should not be quibbling about tithes. We should be desperate to fund the vision of the church, and we should be honoured to be the ATM for the local church when needed.

In 2000, the Lord sent me to Caloundra in Queensland, Australia, to "stand with the pastor and build a mighty church." I thought I had to help build the building because we had recently built a building at the church the Lord was sending me out from.

But within three weeks of arriving here, the very first prophetic word came from the national chairman of all of the Christian Outreach Centre churches in Australia. He said, "You sir, the Lord has shown me there are finances written all over you and you will write six-figure cheques for this church."

Long before the Lord even gave me my broader assignment, He wanted me to get my spiritual covering properly funded and strong. And the reason for this is I could never have built a billion-dollar company without the sophisticated spiritual covering provided by my local church.

I Learnt This Principle the Hard Way in the Special Forces

During the 1970s, I was a member of the elite Rhodesian SAS for four years, and the Selous Scouts for another four years. The Rhodesian army was widely regarded as the finest anti-terrorist force in the world, and the SAS and the Selous Scouts were the two most elite units within the army. However, even they needed a strong "covering." I will use a live operation which we did in 1974 to explain this.

The SAS became aware of a massive armoury being constructed by Russian-trained terrorists over the border in neighbouring Zambia. Zambia was hostile to Rhodesia, and it harboured a massive terrorist army which continuously invaded Rhodesia.

Our job was to cross the Zambezi River, walk the 42 kilometres to the terrorists' base camp and armoury, attack and kill the terrorists, and blow up the armoury. Once we had done that, we needed to get out of there in a hurry before the Zambian Army and Air Force found us.

We arrived at the Zambezi River and set up our HQ on the south bank within Rhodesia. At last light, eight men ferried us across the river in inflatable Zodiacs and then withdrew to the HQ. They were crucial for our urgent recovery back across the river once we had created havoc over in Zambia.

In hindsight, I regard them as akin to the spiritual covering which we value so much today. Keep in mind that this is the Zambezi River, the fourth-largest river in the world—and it was full of huge, hungry crocodiles. Nobody could swim across it! Without our "covering," we would not survive the next two days.

We melted into the night and began our ascent of the imposing Zambezi Escarpment on the Zambian side. Two hours later, when we were halfway up the escarpment, an almighty battle erupted down in the valley behind us. As we stopped and looked back, we could see the green Russian tracer rounds pouring into our HQ, and RPG7 rockets exploding amongst our men as Russian-trained terrorists attacked and overran our "covering."

There was nothing we could do about this, and we simply had to keep going on with the assignment. As we marched through the night, the same thought was on everyone's mind: How will we get back across that great river if our HQ has been taken out? The point is, we had not protected our "covering." We had left it very weak and now we would pay the price, probably with our lives.

We arrived at the terrorist camp at first light and attacked the garrison of terrorists and Zambian soldiers. Then we moved over to the armoury. It was absolutely massive, by far the largest assembly of arms and ammunitions ever encountered during the fourteen-year bush war.

I was in the demolitions team and when we blew this up, it was such a huge explosion that it could be heard over 100 kilometres away. Thereafter, the operation was known as Op Big Bang! The problem was it had woken up the Zambian army. We had truly "poked the bear."

We raced back across 42 kilometres of harsh African bushland, scrambled down the gigantic Zambezi Escarpment, and arrived at the river just after dark, ruing the day we forgot to protect our covering. Fortunately for us, our HQ had managed to radio an SOS to the Rhodesian army just before they were overrun.

> My intercessors alerted me of a pending breakup of our company.

By the time we returned, our army had moved up, counterattacked the terrorists in our basecamp, and had retaken control. They ferried us safely back across the river under cover of darkness.

The most elite unit in the finest antiterrorist force in the world had become so self-confident and cocky that we had forgotten to protect our HQ, our covering, our means of survival. I have never forgotten this and have carried my physical military experience into my spiritual battlefield in the modern marketplace.

What Does This Look Like in Today's Marketplace?

I will close by demonstrating the power of a covering by relating a short story on how my intercessors alerted me of a pending breakup of our company. This warning saved our company and turned it around from a small, $30 million enterprise into the large, influential corporation that it is today.

My intercessors send a prayer report to me every month. One day, I received a prayer report from two of my intercessors. Within the three-page document, they said there was a "parting of the ways" coming at Paladin Corporation—and I had about twelve months to prepare myself for it. Normally, I tabled the prayer reports at the board meetings, but this one was too sensitive, so I stored it in my drawer.

About six months later, another prayer report arrived and in it, the intercessors reminded me of the parting of the ways, which was now about six months away. Again, I filed this in my drawer. While wondering what was going to happen to our business, I began to prepare for any circumstances which could split us up.

And about six months later, one of my two business partners came to me and asked me to buy him out because he did not like the direction in which the company was heading. We had been property developers and were now diversifying into business acquisitions. I immediately realised this was the prophetic word coming into reality, and I agreed to buy him out.

Within two weeks, my other business partner told me he wanted out as well. And I was well enough prepared to buy him out, too. If I had not been forewarned of this, I would not have had the funds to buy them out.

I would have panicked, wondering why they were abandoning the ship, what they knew that I didn't know, and we would have folded. But instead, I was well-prepared and as soon as they left, we grew exponentially into the billion-dollar corporation that we are today. Praise God for spiritual covering!

Conclusion

Dear Pastors, please, *please* consider the concept of providing spiritual covering for your businesspeople. They may not know it, but this is the single biggest blessing you can provide them with, and the fruit you will reap will be massive.

For a more comprehensive video discussion of this topic, please visit the KI Membership website at www.kingdominvestors.com.au, and look under Chapter Lessons for Lessons 16 and 17, which discuss the topic in much more depth. In Lesson 17, I interview my senior pastor to give you an impression of a pastor's point of view, and I also discuss the concept of paid professional intercession. Please take advantage of the seven-day free subscription to watch these videos.

In my opinion, a pastor has the hardest job in the world, and I honour each and every one of you for your service to our Lord and the Kingdom of God.

God bless.

Questions for Reflection and Application

1. David Hodgson describes the confidence that comes from knowing he has a spiritual covering. Pastor, do your businesspeople know that you are holding the rod of God up as they fight against marketplace Amalekites?

2. The author credits the business-nurturing environment in their church with the fact that 10% of the church who are business owners give more than the other 90% of members. Is there a connection between having a business-nurturing environment and having an abundance to fulfill the vision of the church? How can this environment be nurtured?

David Hodgson grew up in Africa during the turbulent 1960s and '70s. He was conscripted into the Rhodesian Army and joined the SAS. He fought behind enemy lines against two armies across three countries for four years.

Thereafter, Dave joined the highly secretive Selous Scouts. He fought undercover with that unit and served as a Tracking and Survival Instructor for a further four years. He left the Special Forces and fought as a mercenary for two years.

Forced to leave Zimbabwe and stateless, Dave became a commercial saturation diver in the oil fields of Southeast Asia and Japan. Eventually he immigrated to Australia, where he came to know the Lord Jesus during an amazing encounter with the Lord at a Reinhard Bonnke Crusade.

Dave is the founder and MD of the Australia-based Paladin Group of Companies. Paladin owns businesses in the mining, telco, construction, IT, health and fitness, financial services, and investment banking arenas. He has businesses in nine countries.

Dave is an influential speaker whose lectures are presented to governments, at conferences, seminars, business groups, churches, Bible colleges, universities, radio, television, and at economic summits all over the world. Dave teaches how he learnt to do God's will God's way, resulting in a meteoric rise from $76,000 in credit card debt and no assets, to a $100 million business in two years and seven months.

In 2007, Dave founded Kingdom Investors (KI) (www.kingdominvestors.com.au), a marketplace ministry which has spread around Australia and Overseas. KI uses its vast marketplace experience to teach Christian businesspeople to multiply their incomes and their influence to be part of a strategic vision to create the world's first "Sheep Nations," as portrayed by Jesus in Matthew 25.

Dave has been married to Merlene for thirty-nine years. They have five adult "children," 11 grandchildren, and one great granddaughter. Dave has attended Empower Church on the Sunshine Coast in Australia for over twenty years.

4
Equipping Worldchangers
Jason Benedict

With the ominous storm clouds of the Emperor Nero's vicious reign of terror filling the horizon, the Apostle Peter wrote these words:

> "But you are a chosen people, a royal priesthood, a holy nation, a people for God's own possession, so that you may proclaim the excellencies of Him who has called you out of darkness into His marvelous light; for you once were not a people, but now you are the people of God... Keep your behavior excellent among the Gentiles, so that in the thing in which they slander you as evildoers, they may because of your good deeds, as they observe them, glorify God on the day of visitation...For such is the will of God, that by doing right you silence the ignorance of foolish people." (1 Peter 2:9–12, 15 NASB)

When you are pastoring day in and day out, preparing for Sundays, putting out fires, dealing with conflicts and a myriad of other mundane pastoral tasks, it's easy to lose sight of the miracle that is the church, and the regal identity of God's people.

It's also easy to lose perspective on the awesome calling and responsibility of pastors. Peter wrote, "shepherd the flock of God." As a pastor, who exactly are you shepherding?

Worldchangers or Refugees?

Who is it that fills your pews on a Sunday morning? Is it a pastor's job to comfort a forlorn and ragtag band of refugees from the big, bad world? Or are we called to equip (raise up) worldchangers? Peter, writing to actual exiles, suffering terrible persecution that was only getting worse, said, "You are a chosen people (nation) a royal priesthood—a nation of the called."

> When you are pastoring day in and day out, it's easy to lose sight of the miracle that is the church.

Peter is referencing a recurring king-priest theme in the old testament. Under Old Testament law, kings and priests typically had different spheres of responsibility, but we see the exceptions of the king-priests: Adam, Melchizedek, and King David operating as types foreshadowing the ultimate King-Priest Jesus.

Jesus commissioned the Church with His kingly authority in Matthew 28 and gave us His mission (c.f. John 20:21: "as the Father has sent Me, so I send you."). On the day of Pentecost, He empowered the fledgling church by sending the Holy Spirit. Anointing this new royal priesthood as tongues of fire rested on each of them the same way His pillar of fire rested on the tabernacle and His shekinah glory rested on Solomon's Temple.

He wanted everyone to understand a new order of priests was being established. Believers are royalty, exercising authority as God's regents and working to reconcile man to God as priests. Pastor, do you realize you are overseeing the training and development of king-priests?

Let me say that again. Pastors and other fivefold equippers are charged with the responsibility of equipping this glorious royal priesthood. This miraculous body of people are otherwise alternatively described in scripture as salt and light, a city set on a hill, the pillar and ground of the truth, ambassadors of reconciliation, the body of Christ, the bride of Christ, and the New Jerusalem.

Why is it important that we get this? This royal priesthood sitting in the collective pews of your city is God's answer to the darkness, brokenness, and suffering in your city!

What are the seemingly insurmountable problems facing your community? Violence, division, perversion, poverty, addiction, joblessness, homelessness, ignorance, and so on. These are the symptoms of broken relationships, principally a broken relationship with God.

Who can change this? Are these challenges too big for God? Do we have any evidence that the church, the body of Christ, has power or authority to make a difference?

What Does the Bible Say?

> "[A]nd what is the incomparable greatness of His power toward us who believe, as displayed in the exercise of His immense strength. This power He exercised in Christ when He raised Him from the dead and seated Him at His right hand in the heavenly realms far above every rule and authority and power and dominion and every name that is named, not only in this age but also in the one to come. And God put all things under Christ's

feet, and gave Him to the church as head over all things. Now the church is his body, the fullness of Him who fills all in all." (Ephesians 1:19–23 NET)

The church is the body of the resurrected, glorified, enthroned King of the universe and all things are under His feet!

In the scripture we began with, Peter is telling the believers they are agents of change—the truth they proclaim (v. 9) and the truth they live (vv. 12, 15)—is transformative. "For such is the will of God, that by doing right you silence the ignorance of foolish people." 2 Peter 2:15 (c.f. 1 Peter 3:16 "that those who slander your good conduct in Christ may be put to shame").

The word *slander* used in this verse is translated various ways: speak evil, slander, falsely accuse, malign, attack, defame, insult. Imagine a church with good works shining so bright (c.f. Matthew 5:16 NKJV) that those who speak against us are ashamed to open their mouths. Wouldn't that be a game-changer?

What does history tell us?

The early church walked in the light of this revelation. Early church congregations found numerous practical ways to be the body of Christ—they established community chests that they used for benevolence of all kinds. Alvin J. Schmidt, in his book *Under the Influence*, credits the early church with pioneering orphanages, hospitals, and schools, for caring for the elderly, freeing slaves, giving dignity to women, elevating sexual morality, and dignifying work.

Reformations such as these flew in the face of pagan norms and turned the world upside down. However, much of the ground gained in the early centuries of the church was lost during the Middle Ages and obscured from view. These truths remained cloistered away for generations but were rediscovered with the reformation.

The reformers discovered the still-glowing embers of our Christian heritage as worldchangers. They not only rekindled the revelation of saving faith, but they also worked tirelessly to transform the world around them. They promoted education—people need to be literate to read their Bibles (*sola scriptura*). They preached and wrote about the value of work and industry.

Luther's teaching on the vocation of the believer as priest kings created the impetus for free market capitalism. Katarina Von Bora, former nun, wife of Martin Luther, and mother of five, was perhaps the foremost Kingdom entrepreneur of the Reformation.

Charged with the upkeep of an abandoned monastery in Wittenberg, she set to work developing an enterprise to support her family and the work of reformation. Her business endeavors included farming, cattle breeding, a hotel and cafeteria, a brewery, a hospital, and numerous real estate deals.

By 1542, the Luthers were the largest landholders in Wittenberg[1]. Her entrepreneurial endeavors and his justification of them may form the backdrop of Luther's theology of enterprise. We know that often more is caught than taught.

---

[1] *This Book Changed Everything: The Bible's Amazing Impact on Our World* by Vishal Mangalwadi, Ashish Alexander, et al. p. 182.

Vishal Mangalwadi credits her demonstration with sowing the seed of biblical entrepreneurship into the hearts of an entire generation of reformers. The reformers' writings went on to sow the seeds of free market capitalism and popular sovereignty that led to new forms of government: economic flourishing and ideas of liberty and justice for all—blessings we are still walking in today.

> Every believer has God-given assignments to fulfill.

This is the heritage of the body of Christ. We need a reformation in our day! The wells dug by our forefathers are still there. The water is still sweet—we simply need to uncap the wells. Pastors, we need to release the river.

Release the River

Earlier in this chapter, I made the bold claim that the solution to the brokenness in your community is sitting in the pews of your church. We have established a scriptural and historical basis for this. But what about practical application in your church? How can we release the untapped potential in the church for revival and reformation in your community?

As pastors, we can make a difference by helping our people grow in a revelation of calling. Every believer has God-given assignments to fulfill. Ask the average believer if they have a calling and you will hear things like, "Well, I once thought I was called to missions," or, "No, I'm just a school principal," "I'm just a contractor," "I'm just a homemaker," and so forth. By and large, they think of calling as something for professional ministers: pastors, evangelists, missionaries, etc. They don't think of themselves as being called.

However, the use of the word calling in reference to fivefold office is rare in the New Testament. Almost every use of the word *calling* is in reference to the believers' calling, our calling to Christ rather than a calling to a task (1 Peter 1:10, 1 Peter 2:9, Ephesians 1:18, Ephesians 4:1, 4, 1 Corinthians 1:26, 2 Thessalonians 1:11). Every single member of your church is called! In fact, a reasonable definition of the word *church* is the community of the called!

Nevertheless, we do see calling used in the sense of task or assignment when Paul speaks of his apostleship: "Paul called to be an apostle." (1 Corinthians 1:1) This other assignment type of calling seems to be a derivative of the first—in other words, the One who called us to Himself gives us assignments.

We see this in the call narratives: Jesus told Peter, Andrew, James, and John, "Come, follow Me, and I will make you fishers of men" (Matthew 4:19). He told Peter, "Feed My sheep." The Lord told Paul that he was given an assignment to preach to gentiles, kings, and Israel (Acts 9:15).

Every believer is called to Christ but beyond that every believer has an assignment or assignments to fulfill. Ephesians 2 describes the fact that God has dreamed a God-sized dream over each of the members in your church; He has good works which He has providentially prepared beforehand.

For we are His workmanship, created in Christ Jesus for good works, which God prepared beforehand so that we would walk in them (Ephesians 2:10).

You can boldly preach next Sunday, the Lord says, "I know the plans I have for you..." (Jeremiah 29:11). It almost sounds cliché—God has a plan for you! But it's revolutionary when 1) people believe they have a God-given assignment, 2) they know what that assignment is, and 3) they have a church that is equipping, sending, and supporting them in that assignment.

> Every single member of your church is called!

Pastor Philip, the senior pastor of an African megachurch, told me about a government official in his congregation. She was so effective in her government role that she had achieved national news recognition for her accomplishments. This is a big deal because this is a place where you don't often hear the words *government* and *effective* in the same sentence. God was obviously at work.

This sister was also a member of the choir and had a lovely voice. He would often thank her for using her singing talent for the glory of God. One day after thanking her for singing, the Lord spoke to him and said, "Why haven't you ever affirmed or encouraged her in her primary assignment in My Kingdom?" At that moment, Philip realized that he thought her Sunday assignment was more important than her Monday assignment.

Ephesians 4:11–12 (NIV) lays out the job description of a five-fold equipper. "So Christ Himself gave the apostles, the prophets, the evangelists, the pastors and teachers, to equip His people for works of service, so that the body of Christ may be built up."

For the average person in your church, what is their work of service? Is it being a greeter, a board member, nursery worker, usher, or Sunday school teacher? Or is it being a plumber, educator, business leader, full-time homemaker, government official, and so forth?

By best estimates, less than 3% of believers are engaged in some form of conventional vocational ministry. This means that 97% have some other primary assignment as their work of service. In other words, their Monday morning assignment is their ministry (work of service).

> As pastors, it's easy to be preoccupied with what takes place within the four walls.

As pastors, it's easy to be preoccupied with what takes place within the four walls. I get it—many volunteer roles go unstaffed; you get a text at 9:30 Sunday morning that the teacher for the toddlers' class is away on vacation. You're out of cups for the church coffee bar. You can't even remember how long it's been since you had a break.

If you pastor a bigger church, maybe it's another set of fires you have to put out. Either way, we must reconcile with the fact that fivefold equippers are meant to equip our members for their Monday morning assignment!

You might say, "But, wait a second. I went to Bible school. I don't know how to equip people for their work, and I can't teach people how to do their job." No worries, you don't have to teach the contractor to build homes or the doctor to treat the sick, or the city council member to govern.

Your role is to equip them to be a faith-filled contractor, a Spirit-filled doctor, or a God-honoring government leader. You can teach them that they have an important assignment in the Kingdom and that their work matters to God. You can develop ways to help every member—from the retired couple to the youth—to identify their gift mix and God-given assignment.

You can help them begin to pray and dream and lean into their work life with a new sense of meaning and significance.

- Teach them to apply the truth of scripture in their work.
- Teach them to serve and lead with the fruit of the Spirit.
- Help them learn to hear the voice of God for themselves, not just in Church but also in the boardroom, classroom, or garage.
- Train them to do spiritual warfare in your community—in whatever place the Lord has given them, and to pray for the Kingdom to come in their organizations, workplaces, and associations.
- In doing this, don't neglect to teach them how to share the gospel in word, deed, and power wherever God has placed them.
- Encourage them and cover them in prayer when they face persecution, trials, and opposition.

You won't have to do this alone; there are people either in your congregation or who the Lord will send you who can provide help with leadership and mentorship. I've seen it time and again. It's like the restaurant owner who we asked to mentor aspiring Christian entrepreneurs.

The opportunity awakened something in him—he came alive. With joyful tears in his eyes, he said, "I never knew I could use my business skills to serve the Lord in this way."

So, you don't need to do vocational training (although I wish the church would lead in this area), and you don't have to do this alone, but many of us as fivefold equippers do need to shift our paradigm to match this biblical expectation. We need to become more intentional about affirming, equipping, and empowering our people for their assignment, and we need to adjust how we define and measure ministry effectiveness to include this.

In the book of Revelation, we see an incredible prophetic picture of the bride of Christ, the New Jerusalem, and the river of life flowing out to touch a sick and broken world.

> "And he showed me a river of the water of life, clear as crystal, coming from the throne of God and of the Lamb, in the middle of its street. On either side of the river was the tree of life, bearing twelve kinds of fruit, yielding its fruit every month; and the leaves of the tree were for the healing of the nations." (Revelation 22:1, 2, c.f. Hebrews 12:22)

John is picking up the same river theme that he spoke of in his Gospel, a theme foreshadowed in Eden, in Ezekiel and Zechariah. The one who believes in Me, as the Scripture said, 'From his innermost being will flow rivers of living water.'" But this He said in reference to the Spirit, whom those who believed in Him were to receive; for the Spirit was not yet given, because Jesus was not yet glorified. (Matthew 7:38)

Again, a life-giving river flowing from the people of God into a broken world bringing life and healing. How much the revival river in your church is flowing is going to be measured more by people being equipped and released into their assignment than by goosebumps on a Sunday!

Picture janitors, mayors, teachers, pastors, doctors, nurses, salespeople, and students—each of them a mobile temple with the river flowing from their innermost being. Each of them is equipped in their local church to be a point of contact between heaven and earth.

> If your light is confined in the four walls, it doesn't matter how salty we are—the world doesn't care.

For this biblical vision to be realized, the church must become expert in equipping every member to be salt and light.

Salt and Light

In Matthew 5, Jesus describes believers as the salt of earth and the light of the world. The Lord is telling us that we as believers must be both distinctive (salty savor) and present (not hidden, under a basket). You have to have both for this to work because if we don't taste any different than the world, then our presence is insignificant. If we aren't present, if your light is confined in the four walls, then it doesn't matter how salty we are—the world doesn't care.

The car salesman who has a little fish printed on his business card but ripped me off is present, but the saltiness of

Christ is missing. On the other hand, someone who is full to overflowing with the Word of God and the Spirit of God, but who keeps that compartmentalized to a couple of hours on Sunday morning, has their light under a basket.

This scripture helps us understand how it is that some of our most broken and bankrupt communities also have some of the highest church attendance. You would think that wherever the gospel goes and people pray the sinner's prayer, it would bring societal transformation. The Bible tells us to expect transformation. In history, we see the impact of Gospel transformation.

In the first book of the Bible, the Lord gives us a template for transforming the world. It's so simple we might miss it, but so important that we see it repeated throughout scripture.

Most theologians believe Genesis 3 implies that God and man walked together in the garden in the cool of the day. This is revolutionary—if you want to change the world, walk daily with God, listen to His voice, and do what He tells you to do.

I imagine Adam and God walking in the garden and talking about this or that crop, this or that animal. I believe Adam was receiving instructions from the Lord about how to manage his responsibilities in their agricultural partnership.

The pattern is repeated throughout scripture. Enoch, Noah, Abraham, Moses, David, Jesus, and the New Testament apostles all modeled this Eden pattern of walking with God. Here it is again.

The 3 I's

Intimacy: Walk in daily intimacy with the Lord.

Instruction: Seek specific wisdom, revelation, and instruction for your assignment and responsibilities.

Implementation: Total obedience, do what he tells you to do.

When I share this simple pattern with believers in the marketplace, I see the lights come on. It's not uncommon for people to say, "Wow, I have a devotional life, but unless there's a crisis, I don't really seek the Lord specifically for work. Which vendor to go with, how to solve the cash flow problem, which resume to move to the top of the stack.

Through informal poll-taking on my part, I would surmise that nine out of ten church members don't have a revelation of their Monday morning assignment in Christ. As a result, they are not fully engaged with the Kingdom in their work life. This disengagement is keeping the river from flowing in our communities, and their churches are not helping.

Pastor, in your defense, pastors are not trained for this, and we don't have many working examples of this. Our existing templates for ministry don't really include this. The culture of our denominations and church networks don't encourage it, for the most part.

So how do we move the needle? Here are some ideas:

- **Prayer**: Pastors, pray for your people to be activated in their assignments, and to get a revelation of what the Lord has called them to. Encourage your people to begin workplace prayer meetings where possible. Solicit work-related prayer requests specifically wherever you ask for prayer requests. Add marketplace transformation to the prayer agenda at weekly church prayer meetings. Do altar ministry—pray for people to be raised up as entrepreneurs, promoted in their jobs, for jobs to be created and wealth released for Kingdom purposes.

- **The Sunday service**: Preach it! Earlier in this chapter, there is a bulleted list of things you can do and teach. You have service at least 52 times a year (possibly much more). Touch on this in every service in some way. Preach an entire message on calling, assignment, work life, work as worship and such topics two to four times a year, but touch on it all the time. If your paradigm as a preacher shifts, it will begin to come out in your weekly preaching. When people in the congregation have victories and breakthroughs in their Monday assignment, have them give testimonies; you may need to solicit this initially, but it will snowball.

- **Leadership**: Cast vision, meet with your elders and ministry leaders, and begin to talk about the biblical expectation here. Maybe schedule an offsite meeting or retreat to launch this. Appoint leaders to carry the torch in this area, such as a marketplace leader or pastor. That being said, avoid just making this a compartmentalized department. Ask leaders of every department to integrate this understanding of assignment into what they are doing: worship, Sunday school, youth, and so on.

- **Measure**: Adjust your definition of the win to include equipping and sending worldchangers and community transformation. Adopt metrics to measure these actions and results.

- **Equipping**: Establish special equipping opportunities for your members—include faith at work in your children's and adult education and discipleship programs.

Pastor, fivefold equipper, I pray that the Lord gives you grace and wisdom to activate the dormant king-priests in your congregation to turn the world upside down!

Questions for Reflection and Application

1. The author says those sitting in the pews of your church are "God's answer to the brokenness in your community." If you had to rate your congregation's awareness of this fact from 1 (aware) to 10 (fully aware), how would you rate them? What could you do to awaken the dormant Worldchangers?

2. The author gives evidence that previous generations of the Church had a better understanding of the royal priesthood's role and the responsibility to work as worldchangers. What could you do to help uncap the wells of revelation?

3. The author wrote, "(Pastor), you won't have to do this alone; there are people either in your congregation or who the Lord will send you who can provide help with leadership and mentorship." Can you think of anyone who could help you? Create a list.

Jason Benedict is an entrepreneur and innovator in business and world missions. He and his wife, Kimberly, work to train and mobilize global church movements with a focus on world missions, Kingdom business, and education.

Jason has served as a strategist at the Regent University Center for Entrepreneurship since 2008. He is also the CEO of a management consulting firm he founded in 2009 to help entrepreneurs succeed in life and business.

5
Getting a Vision—Awakened to Dream

Svetlana Papazov

Eight-year-old Jeremiah sported fashionable, orange-colored hair, and had come with his mother to Real Life Church. I enjoyed the controlled chaos and especially the bobbing heads of kids exchanging pictures, crayons, and stories in our KidPreneurs camp—an incubator for children five to twelve in which they explored God's purpose for their lives through entrepreneurship.

Everyone was engaged except for Jeremiah. He wasn't searching for colorful pictures, cutting, or gluing like the other kids. He only stared at the poster paper in front of him—not a single picture glued, not a single word spelling out his dream.

Much younger kids were already cutting shapes and drawing their squiggly lines, laughing, and gluing pictures of beaches, mansions, and lemonade stands. But Jeremiah seemed paralyzed by the assigned task—to simply dream.

I knelt beside him and asked, "What is your hope for the future, my friend? What are your dreams?"

He looked at me and said bluntly, "I'm not dreaming about anything."

Jeremiah, like many of the other kids there that day, came from some rough circumstances and lived in an economic desert, disconnected from hope in a society and a God who cared. This is why we were here. This was our purpose.

I tried again. "What I'm saying is, what are the things that you really want to share with your friends?"

He said, "I don't want to do any of that."

I wasn't sure if I could awaken the dreamer in him, but I ventured one more time. "Listen, when you play, do you like sports?"

He looked at me and said, "Uh, I kind of like sports and kind of don't because when it rains and the fields get muddy, I can't play football."

> Hope for the future was being birthed, and an entrepreneurial mindset was emerging.

A thought came to mind, and I went with it. "Oh, the fields! The fields are muddy and stopping you from playing, right?" He nodded. "How would you like to solve that problem—to play even when it has rained? Don't you think many people will be grateful that you thought of a better way?"

For the first time, he looked at me with interest. "Uh-huh."

A deep sense of relief came over me. "How about if you and I dream of something to put down so that when it rains, you and your friends can play? Kind of like that green outdoor carpet." I pointed to the greenish-colored carpet in the other room.

Jeremiah's face lit up. He didn't need my help anymore. He took the magazines and began to look for green stuff, carpets, and things that he could cut, paste, and draw. Jeremiah's vision was unleashed. His blank poster now burst with colorful pieces of his imagination.

Hope for the future was being birthed, and an entrepreneurial mindset was emerging. Because, to think entrepreneurially, all a person needs to do is to come up with a viable solution to a problem.

Dr. Douglas Melton, Director for the Entrepreneurial Engineering Program at The Kern Family Foundation, says that a person with an entrepreneurial mindset is an agent of change and designs the world of tomorrow. God strategically positions believers for influence in business, education, government, media, arts and entertainment, family, and religion. Then God sends us on His mission as agents of change in the world around us.

God, the Ultimate Entrepreneur who has fashioned everything out of nothing, has formed everyone uniquely in order to co-create with Him redeemed futures for humanity (Jeremiah 29:11). If we pay attention to the beckoning of the Holy Spirit, we can act in an entrepreneurial manner and partner with God in His work in the world.

I have come to understand that the church cannot transform its communities if it stays disengaged from society, playing "church" with its own Lego blocks. If you are reading this book, I'm sure you agree and are one of the change agents I'm describing.

The body of Christ is called to be a living, prophetic, tangible model of the Great Commission. That statement is one you've, no doubt, read before. However, the second part of that statement is one you may not have heard, and it is what this book is about—the church is called to be a living, prophetic, tangible model of the Great Commission by integrating faith, creativity, and mission in the marketplace.

When we disciple people for the whole of life, we usher godly transformation into all spheres of society. Thankfully, the churches that are missionally engaging their communities are on the rise. If your church hasn't started on that journey yet, don't fret. You can retool what you are already doing to be more impactful as a missional instrument in the marketplace.

> A church that trains for mission-at-work is not a "how" church but a "why" church.

The New Testament church saw itself as a disruptor. It accepted the call of Jesus to enter all sectors of society across the world, not just on Sunday but also on Monday, in order to share the gospel with love and courageous innovation.

Following the New Testament model, the contemporary church should be emboldened to live faithfully for Christ in the public arena, not because everyone understands the church, but because the church understands the need of everyone: a need of a Savior from a wrecked existence and a need of a Healer from human suffering.

After more than a decade serving as a full-time pastor and equipping different churches for mission in the marketplace, I have observed that a church that trains for mission-at-work and closes the perilous Sunday-to-Monday gap is not a "how" church but a "why" church.

That type of church has a mindset that is not about methodology, but about the praxis of Christology, about modeling itself after "The Word became flesh and blood, and moved into the neighborhood" (John 1:14 MSG), in order to practice a corporate, contextualized expression of the Great Commission.

This kind of mindset helps churches love their cities well through three priorities: first, translating the gospel for those who we'll call the unchurched—those who have little or no church experience; second, deploying disciples who attend to the whole of life in all sectors of society; and third, strategically placing disciples in the marketplace to impact the economic health of their communities.

Churches wanting to lead entrepreneurially in the mission of God and become an integral part of society prepare themselves on Sunday to bridge their faith into the workweek on Monday. What if your church were to fully embrace this vision and train the Jeremiahs of all ages, young and old, to dream, create, and contribute? What if the neighborly love your church professes found an economic aspect and pushed into the mission field of the marketplace on the outside of your church walls?

There is already a burgeoning number of churches embedded in the economy. But what will happen if more local churches awaken to the necessity of establishing its faithful presence in the marketplace? We know people spend the majority of their time outside of church each week.

What if the church was present during those hours? Can the church meet the curiosity of our next generation with environments that dare them to dream and create? We unleashed our members to equip our children—the future of our society, especially in economically vulnerable communities—to dream, create, and contribute to this future?

According to the Barna Research Group, the time before the age of thirteen is when people are most prone to accept and act upon the salvation message. The future of the American Church and our nation hinges on reaching our children with a holistic gospel. For that matter, the future of any nation depends on how well it reaches their next generation for Jesus Christ.

As I watched Jeremiah awaken the dreams within him as he sought to solve a problem he understood in his own community, I imagined him one day walking the hallways of his high school, confident in his human dignity and entrepreneurial mindset. Can you see the hallways of your city's high school bursting at the seams with graduates ready to dream, create, and contribute to society just like Jeremiah?

Can you see the potential for the spiritual, economic, and social lift both in vulnerable and economically developed communities if your church enters them on a holistic mission? Jesus says that the Father is always working (John 5:17).

His creative and redeeming work is needed both in poverty-stricken and in wealthy countries. What would it take to unleash the potential of creative, working Jeremiahs, young and old, across our nation and beyond in a relationship with a creative Christ?

Living the Dream

Like young Jeremiah, I too grew up in the bondage of a spiritual, entrepreneurial, and economic desert—although I lived behind the Iron Curtain where entrepreneurs were punished by law. My mom was one of them. But in His grace, God unleashed my imagination through one of my professors who stirred within me a hunger for more.

When I heard of the freedom those in the United States had, I knew I had to get there. Through hard work, my quest for free expression of the human spirit eventually brought me to the U.S. Once here, I immediately started my own business of a design-build firm utilizing my graduate degree in landscape architecture.

The first business was such a success that my husband, Michael, and I opened three more—a garden center, florist shop, and a gift store. Yet, I still carried my youthful dream to finish a biblical degree, a dream unattainable in Communist countries.

So, once we were financially stable, I took full advantage of this American opportunity and furthered my education at Christian institutions by finishing a second Master's in Theology, and a Doctorate of Ministry in Leadership.

As I worked, I realized that not everyone saw the gift of freedom to create as the God-calling that I did. I was puzzled by the way in which followers of Christ casually approached this opportunity to co-create with God. I knew I had a unique perspective, coming from a place where what American Christians took for granted was outlawed.

So, the Lord led my husband and me into church leadership, and I transitioned from a businesswoman into an ordained minister. We determined our focus would be on connecting our members to God's plan to integrate work and faith—doing real life with real people, connecting them to the real God in order to see a spiritual, social, and economic transformation not just on Sunday, but also on Monday and throughout the week.

During my first pastorate at a large church in the Dallas, Texas, metroplex, I was privileged to work with ethnically diverse, vision-driven believers who, although living in scarcity, didn't allow that to limit or define God's plan for them. These people became our Jeremiahs.

As we worked side by side, I soon saw the needs in this community were not just spiritual. Many in the community were living in survival mode. They needed good jobs, but some had criminal records, and many lacked the education or skills needed to secure stable, better-paying employment. I knew I couldn't stay on the sidelines when it came to their work situation and only speak about the matters of their spirit—for me, it all went together.

My decision to help came in the form of education and encouragement. I began by turning Wednesday night services into training sessions, where I taught the biblical concepts of leadership, entrepreneurship, and economics, sharing with our congregation the same principles I taught as a professor in the business department of a Christian university in town.

During that time, our congregation grew. People's entrepreneurial skills increased as they prayed, explored God-sized visions for their lives, and learned valuable steps in how to open a business. There were many Jeremiahs that experienced upward mobility—some found employment and better jobs, while others started their own businesses.

Still today, I treasure a note I received from a young Hispanic couple that came faithfully to these midweek services. When they started their own business, they sent a message to express gratitude for the way the church loved them.

We were concerned for their family's economic life and gave them practical help to improve their living conditions and their place in society. Now, this couple is a tangible representation of the love of God in the marketplace as business owners who train students in job skills for the dental industry.

During my second pastorate at a well-established, mid-size church in Maryland sixty miles from Washington, D.C., I saw similar economic needs in the surrounding community. The Holy Spirit impressed me to reach out to local schools in these distressed areas so my team and I could work with families.

We knew that while helping parents improve the quality of their lives, we could also train the children in skills needed for their schoolwork. We found a school full of Jeremiahs, young and old, who welcomed our church to lead them toward an economic lift. Our church volunteers were allowed to work with the parents and students on the school premises after school hours.

My vision was to bridge the gap of the secular and sacred divide through a Faith and Public School Partnership Prototype, which our team developed. We used this program to train students and parents in employability skills, financial savviness, and goal-setting.

The Partnership Prototype's structure centered upon two foundational modules: a development track and a transformational track. The development track addressed the social and economic lift, whereas the transformational track addressed the spiritual change in the participants.

In the development track for adults, we taught goal-setting, financial intelligence, and job readiness courses. The children's curriculum included fun activities and biblical instruction that followed the adults' curriculum thematically to facilitate common family discussions on financial stewardship and life's goals. The development track was a way to build the bridge to the community and lift it economically, while the transformational track made the pivotal difference in people's spiritual state.

The transformational track consisted of three main elements: intercessory prayer, Christian value-based curricula, and relational connectors. Perhaps the most important aspect of our program was prayer. Before our weekly training, our volunteers walked the school, praying. In addition, other church intercessors prayed for the school throughout the week.

Christian values undergirded all curricula, and one-on-one relationships were formed with the participants. Intentionally, several of the volunteers attended the instructions not as facilitators but as connectors—becoming friends with the parents. Because we shaped relationships, many came to our Sunday services, and several accepted Christ.

After we'd been at the school for six months, training and supporting both the parents and the students, the assistant principal told us that they could sense the entire atmosphere of the school changing. In addition, the parents who were participating in our partnership prototype began to ask us how they could help their neighbors as we had helped them.

During my years as a small business owner, I had become keenly aware that most of my clients never asked themselves which local church they will go to on Sunday morning. Talking about church and God were conversations that many of them carefully avoided.

Since then, the desire to find effective ways for the church to reconnect—or possibly connect for the first time—

unchurched people to God has been my ministry goal. Right before I transitioned from a small business owner to a pastor, during a lengthy session of prayer, I had a vision of something that on the outside looked like businesses, but on the inside looked like a church.

It was a vision of the marketplace, and the church was placed in the middle of it. What God showed me was a confirmation of what I had begun to understand—that whole-life discipleship integrates faith into work and economics.

> God showed me that whole-life discipleship integrates faith into work and economics.

If we separate biblical principles such as creativity, human dignity, and stewardship from the workplace, we set our cities up for failure. Although I had never seen anything like my vision, I knew that God was calling my husband and me to meld church and work, economics and entrepreneurship in a practical way. I faithfully applied these concepts in my pastorates in Texas and Maryland and in the founding and pastoring of an entrepreneurial church in Virginia.

In order to close the Sunday-to-Monday gap between church and the marketplace in a way that would allow us to duplicate, my husband and I, along with a team of supporters, started Real Life Church. Our team is doing missional work among businesses and entrepreneurs.

In our desire to be embedded in the economy of our city, and bridge the sacred and secular divide in a practical way, Real Life Church opened Real Life Center for Entrepreneurial and

Leadership Excellence—a business incubator that prepares people for their occupations. The Entrepreneurial Center trains in leadership and entrepreneurship to give unchurched people the opportunity to experience God and faith outside of Sunday as we lift our community economically, socially, and spiritually.

We care for our community and contribute to our local economy by guiding people to identify and develop their gifts and skills in order to lead well at their jobs, hire new employees, or start new businesses. In addition, we do business incubation.

We also offer co-working space and private offices for work, business consulting, networking to identify new job opportunities, educational workshops, and adult and next-generation entrepreneurial training. Most of these functions are facilitated by church volunteers skilled to equip in these various ways.

We have found that developing people's entrepreneurial skills sets them up for success and unleashes their potential. Having a problem-solving mentality and a growth-oriented mindset allows one to do well anywhere: at home, at school, at work, in government, and in business. For that reason, we have created faith and entrepreneurship programs for kids, teens, and adults.

The programs of Real Life KidPreneurs and Real Life TeenPreneurs as summer camps, Beyond VBS, and school classroom curricula have been effective in fostering next-generation creativity. The Real Life AdultPreneurs program trains in business and entrepreneurial skills for adults interested in starting their own businesses and also for those affected by the opioid crisis and who are in at-risk situations. During our Kid, Teen, and

AdultPreneurs programs, we have repeatedly discovered and unleashed our Jeremiahs to dream, create, and contribute.

Although our real estate has a small footprint, we believe we can make a big difference with it. Real Life's small building of 3,200 square feet has provided co-working space and offices for more than a dozen businesses.

One such business owner is Pam, a financial professional who came to us when she couldn't afford her own building. The local coffee shops no longer fit her clients' needs. She was in that in-between stage where many entrepreneurs do not make it.

The Real Life incubator supports entrepreneurs by offering private offices in vulnerable times of too-fast growth and not enough capacity. In our facilities and in our programs, Pam has found a place to belong, grow, and steward hundreds of thousands of dollars for her clients. She has hired four employees, and her impact on the economy has increased because Real Life supports small business owners with entrepreneurial environments and low-cost rent.

In addition to offering private offices, we facilitate business training based on biblical principles. Hundreds of adult entrepreneurs have been trained at Real Life through workshops, masterminds, business coaching, networking, and caring relationships.

In this way, we empower for greater contribution to our local economy. Moreover, we have unleashed the imaginations of hundreds of children through the Real Life Kid-Preneurs and TeenPreneurs programs.

Spurred into creativity, Zoe and her older sister, Chloe, launched a small business that they called Knicks and Knacks after finishing the Real Life KidPreneurs summer camp. Together, they have developed a line of goods with teens and preteens in mind. These are two young entrepreneurs who are not waiting to become adults in order to dream, create, and contribute to our local economy.

> In our training, we focus on developing an entrepreneurial mindset with a biblical worldview.

In all of our training, we focus on developing an entrepreneurial mindset with a biblical worldview. We teach that business dreams can have a social and economic impact on the real world and the real economy. We help adults and kids reverse engineer their dreams into strategic business plans that they can launch now.

The majority of the people in our church startup have joined because of faith and entrepreneurship integration. Kelly, a digital marketing expert, reconnected to God and faith and is now a committed member of our church because she was looking for a space to expand her business and rented an office at Real Life.

Liza came to our Christmas Small Business Open House Expo as a vendor. The next Sunday, she came to church and recommitted her life to Christ. Now her kids, too, have become a part of the church.

Terry is a freelance photographer who one Sunday came on our property to take pictures of his client. As my husband and I approached him, he thought he would get in trouble for trespassing. To his surprise, we welcomed him to utilize not just the outside of our property, but the business incubator as well, by doing photo shoots in one of our vacant offices.

That deeply impacted him, and Terry and his wife came back to Real Life, this time to church, and there they found a genuine church family that has welcomed them home. Terry's photography business has also expanded since joining our Real Life church community.

These are only a few of the many lives that have been touched through Real Life's integration of faith and entrepreneurship.

Patient Work With Lasting Impact

As grateful as we are for each individual transformation, and as rewarding as the work of faith integration is, the Real Life Church has experienced steady but, what would seem to most, slow growth. Although we minister through entrepreneurial events, workshops, networking, coaching, and consulting, this work is not a convert-producing machine.

As a church planter, I was tempted to compare the attendance numbers of our organic church start to the attendance numbers of some who had made national headlines as fast-growing church plants that began with lots of money and big groups of transfer Christians. Although in the first three years we experienced more than fifty-five salvations, I considered our attendance numbers to be a failure. That was until I reminded myself to be patient and see our work for what it is—a missionary work.

We are not reaching practicing Christians or church hoppers; we are reaching the lapsed and nonchurched. I call them "nones"—people who are away from God and church.

Barna identifies the lapsed as people who have not been in church for more than a month (our own experience is that they have not been in church for several years, with the exception of holidays) and of whom only 4% consider their faith very important. The nones do not identify with any faith, or if they do, it is not Christian.

What we have found out is that people who have not been in church for years, or never, are slow to warm up to the gospel and need time to make a lasting decision for Christ. To encourage my heart, for a season I had to stop counting Sunday numbers and refocus my attention on counting the numbers we were reaching in the Sunday-to-Monday connect bridge. This simple act reframed my thinking about our church's scorecard.

If someone is looking for a fast church-growth model, the entrepreneurial church is not it. There is nothing fast when we are building Church for Monday. This church must be thoughtful and patient in order to effect lasting transformation; otherwise, people begin to feel bulldozed into grace and will reject our witness. Personally, I see this approach as closer to God's intent than impressive numbers generated by well-financed starts populated by believers transferring from established churches.

As word got out about what we were doing, churches, organizations, universities, church planting networks, and denominational districts started reaching out for training and coaching in translating the gospel for the unchurched, in equipping believers for whole-life discipleship, and in strategic envisioning for embedding churches in the marketplace for economic impact.

Because of the extensive work I've done in the faith and work arena, the Made to Flourish organization—a nationwide network that empowers pastors and their churches to integrate faith, work, and economic wisdom for the flourishing of their communities—felt that my experience would be of value to their East Coast network in Richmond, Virginia. Made to Flourish asked me to be its representative as City Network Leader there.

In addition, I serve as faculty at the Acton University—a unique annual forum of thousands of global leaders from over ninety countries that gather to explore the intersection between faith and the marketplace.

Giving leadership to the Richmond Made to Flourish network, teaching at Acton University, training and coaching for organizations such as Church Multiplication Network, Mosaix, and other forerunners in the faith integration movement has been rewarding work. It presents me with the opportunity not only to equip leaders but also to learn from the mavericks' novel ways to bridge the marketplace gap.

I believe that if the church embeds itself in the community as the incarnate love of Christ, it will see the Jeremiahs waiting to be reached. I pray the following questions stir your heart and mind:

Where are your Jeremiahs? Are you entering their economic gates? How are you and your church creatively engaging them?

The Scorecard

An Example to Follow

W. E. H. Lecky says the moral influence of Jesus's teachings on the Western world was the most powerful moral lever that has ever been applied to the affairs of man.[2] This new way of life challenged all human cultures. In this present age, we see only partial transformation; neither all world cultures nor every person in a group culture will align with the authority of King Jesus before the Second Coming.

Nevertheless, among those who accept His reign, the Spirit of God forms a transformed community, which in turn goes on to transform societies. Thus, the church becomes a sign, symbol, and foretaste of God's redeeming love in real neighborhoods, bearing witness to a new way of being human.

Jesus continuously challenged the religious leaders of His day to understand the Law was not given to restrict people in their basic tasks, but to encourage them to live in harmony with one another and with God. Twenty-one centuries later, the challenge to church leaders remains the same—answer in love.

When going after the Great Commission, do not forget the Great Commandment. A church that is preparing to embed itself in the marketplace for culture formation needs to be transformed itself and pay close attention to the attitude of the heart, because this is what ultimately matters.

---

[2] W. E. H. Lecky, *History of European Morals from Augustus to Charlemagne*, 3rd. rev. ed. (New York: Appleton, 1916), 338.

We must love our neighbor, as Jesus loved us—from the heart and 'til the end (John 13:34). If we only do outreach programs for the sake of our scorecard, then we are not doing it for the sake of our neighbor.

> Justification depends on God's mercy to the repentant and not on the works of the repentant.

Before we reach sinful people outside the church, let's make them a place to belong with forgiven people inside the church. Let's remember that justification depends on the mercy of God to the repentant and not on the works of the repentant. When Zacchaeus restored his ill-gotten gains, this did not precede but followed his acceptance by Jesus (Luke 19:1–10).

Chances are none of us got into leadership in order to see our churches stop reaching new people and stop accomplishing God's mission. But almost every church in our Western culture is challenged to navigate the new trends of a post-Christian society.

For churches who realize that new times call for new methods, I suggest we re-envision Jesus's first-century method for today's twenty-first-century church. As we are revamping our churches' track record, can we do it by keeping in mind the three *S's* that Jesus practiced regularly (Luke 19:1–10)?

- Seek
- See
- Sit

Jesus went out to *seek* the lost in the middle of their marketplace activities. Of the fifty-two parables Jesus told, forty-five had a workplace context.[3] Jesus himself spent His adult life in the profession of a carpenter. It is in the marketplace where He was able to see Peter and Andrew, James and John, Zacchaeus, Levi, the centurion, the woman at the well, and so many others.

Then He joined them to sit at their table to listen to their brokenness in order to offer His redeeming solution to their pain. No wonder so many who felt they were outcasts felt they belonged in Jesus's company.

What if our church activities centered on the priorities Jesus centered His on, so we can see results Jesus saw? Seek out the marketplace Zacchaeuses as Jesus did, see them as Jesus did, sit at their table as Jesus did—*before* they believe and repent, as Zacchaeus did.

In an experience-oriented, high-touch, post-truth world, where many look for spirituality, but not Christianity, the Holy Spirit empowers the church to contextualize its witness for cultural application. The spiritual climate in North America and the West allows for many religious thoughts to exist together.

If in this new landscape, local churches **seek** out their communities by familiarizing themselves with their pains and joys, **see** the people and people groups affected by brokenness, and **sit** at the community's table not as "the know it all," but as "I

---

[3] Umidi, Joseph, *Transformational Coaching: Bridge Building that Impacts, Connects, and Advances the Ministry and the Marketplace* (Fairfax, VA: Xulon Press, 2005), 195.

want to hear it all," in order to gain society's ear, then they'll be able to bridge the Sunday-to-Monday gap.

They'll get the response that Zacchaeus gave—repent and believe. If we assume the humble posture of an explorer of the marketplace, then we can revamp the church's focus to reflect the heart of God for our postmodern neighbor.

The Scorecard

It is not possible to unpack the depth of the scorecard for the Church for Monday in one chapter. This topic deserves an entire book. Here I will outline with broad strokes some important points about what to measure and how to measure the components of the scorecard in order to begin the conversation.

When talking about the scorecard, there is a question to consider: "Are you willing to shift from a church-centric scorecard to a Kingdom-centric scorecard?" And another important one: "Are you willing to expand what you celebrate?" Unless we see the value of measuring impact beyond the Sunday gathering, we won't be willing to envision new ways of what and how we measure.

Most churches have a scorecard that measures how well our congregations do on Sunday and not how well our congregants do on Monday. This has to change if we want to change how well the church does in the marketplace. Not only do we have to connect Sunday to Monday, but we also need to bring Monday back to Sunday.

What I mean is the gathered experience on Sunday needs to focus on equipping believers for the scattered Monday mission, which is to oversee how God's Kingdom shows up on earth in our own communities amid societal ills.

The church is present in the world not to build itself, but to build the Kingdom of God in the marketplace and to bring people into a life-giving experience with King Jesus. We are commissioned to steward God's redeeming presence for our communities when whole-life disciples embedded in the economy prayerfully seek God's wisdom at work while solving a financial crisis with a client.

Or this occurs when they offer an innovative design that has stumped the creative team, or when they mitigate in a peaceful manner amid a high-strung, nerve-wracking case that ushers God's Kingdom and redeeming presence, and translates the gospel for the unchurched by conveying Christ's love to them.

Jesus was sharply focused on the Kingdom of God. During His earthly ministry, He talked about the Kingdom of God and the Kingdom of heaven over 100 times and only once about the church on the backdrop of the Kingdom of heaven.[4]

Our scorecard must reflect how the church expands the territories of God's Kingdom in the marketplace, or it won't have the right parameters. The role of the local church and every function it performs is pivotal for the life of the community because it ushers in the Kingdom of God as the source of all life.

Nothing can substitute that role and the foretaste it brings. No social services, government programs, or civil groups can restore the broken lives in our communities as does the King

---

[4] McNeal, Reggie. "3 Epic Shifts Underway in the Church" filmed 2019. YouTube Video, 4:13. Posted 2019.
https://youtu.be/MT54Q73dnD4 (accessed June 27, 2019).

of the heavenly Kingdom that works through His church anywhere the church engages the life of the community.

For that reason, it is imperative that we get outside of our church-centric bubble and connect to the marketplace in meaningful ways to bring to it the fullness of life as Jesus intended people to have.

Pastors, we are entrusted with Jesus's flock to equip them for the majority, not just the minority, of their life wherever it takes them outside of the church walls. Will you join me in recalibrating our church's scorecard to reflect the biblical conviction of whole-life discipleship both as a gathered and a scattered church, bringing the Kingdom of God amid a broken marketplace?

Beyond the 3 B's: Bodies, Bucks, and Buildings

Regardless of what else makes the list of a church's parameters, and how intentional, or lapsed the church is in measuring results, three things are ever-present on any church's scorecard—the 3 B's: bodies, bucks, and buildings. The question is, "Are these parameters sufficient for the Church for Monday Scorecard, or should we go beyond them?"

As measuring church success has always revolved around those three (sometimes expressed as the church's ABCs—attendance, buildings, and cash), how much do they matter? Are they the "holy trinity" for a local church? Kind of, yes.

Before you start throwing rocks and scriptures at me, you should know I am the last person to be taken over by practicality. I usually function in a big-picture capacity, focused on trends and seeing future realities decades before they happen. Details like how many people it will take to achieve the vision and how much money it will cost usually come second to me.

But not to my MBA-trained husband, who stewards millions of dollars through his marketplace vocation and is detail-oriented in personality. To him, all of my church-dreaming has always translated into bodies, bucks, and buildings. In God's providential wisdom, I am partnered with someone who keeps the practical side of things on the front burner.

So, I understand the need for strong numbers of bodies, bucks, and buildings. Without a comprehensive vision of biblically faithful, theologically informed, and missionally aligned 3 B's, we will be stuck in the red with the accounting books. Measuring matters, but what we measure and *why* we measure it matters more.

What Do We Measure?

We need to define the *it*, or we will never hit it. I tell the entrepreneurs that I business-consult that unless they have a clear vision of their future enterprise and then reverse engineer a pathway to it, they will never get there.

When an entrepreneur starts a business, they must picture the mature business in full. And then they must chart a path to it with obtainable and measurable first and next steps that lead to their desired destination, not to someone else's. Otherwise, their startup is only going to confirm the statistic that 90% of small businesses fail in the first five years."[5]

Vision is also important to the pastor and the success of their church. Without a God-breathed, clear vision for the

---

[5] Neil Patel, "90% of Startups Fail: Here's What You Need to Know About the 10%," Forbes.com, Jan. 16, 2015.
http://www.forbes.com/sites/neilpatel/2015/01/16/90-of-startups-will-fail-heres-what-you-need-to-know-about-the-10/#4d5d7cbe55e1 (accessed July 11, 2019).

church's DNA—its unique place in the global body of Christ, growth structure, and supporting systems—the local church may also find itself becoming a grim statistic.

Let's envision the future of the church so we can reverse engineer a pathway to it. The *it* is a church embedded in the marketplace, making not only a lasting spiritual but also a socioeconomic difference as well. This type of vision cannot be measured with a church-centric scorecard.

That scorecard is only concerned with how well the congregation is doing on Sunday, but it hasn't expanded its categories to measure how well the congregants do on Monday. A new Kingdom-centric scorecard is needed to measure how the gathered experience prepares the scattered church for mission at work and the practice of whole-life discipleship.

In addition to the gathered experience, measuring and celebrating impact beyond Sunday is what the revamped scorecard must reflect. Measuring the 3 B's for your scattered church marketplace impact, the Sunday-to-Monday Connect Bridge, and Integration Onramps must garner the same passion and adequate budget as measuring the 3 B's for Sunday. This is only a segment of what comprises our Real Life Scorecard, but this offers a glimpse of the priorities we measure:

Bodies
- Salvations
- Water baptisms
- Miraculous physical healings
- Households ministered through church services
- Unchurched households reached Monday to Sunday
- Sunday guests/co-workers of church members
- Employment opportunity assistance of church families

- Upward mobility of church families
- Increased revenue of the Real Life Entrepreneurs
- Scaled businesses of the Real Life Entrepreneurs
- Entrepreneurs ministered through the entrepreneurial center
- Kids ministered through the entrepreneurial youth programs
- Teens ministered through the entrepreneurial youth programs
- Local pastors and Christian entrepreneurs equipped for marketplace ministry

Budget

- Tithes, offerings, rental space, and additional creative revenue steams
- Scholarships for kids and teens, and entrepreneurial youth programs
- Fundraising for faith-based entrepreneurial training

Building

- Networking events, business meetups, community workshops, financial training, private offices, co-working space, event space, and retreats.

What are your priorities that your church's scorecard measures? Because we defined the *it* to be a church embedded in the marketplace, let's envision it. When reverse engineering a vision, the following elements are key:

- **Envision the mature vision**

It is important that we envision in full, as much as we can master, the mature and not the infancy stage of an endeavor, in order to shoot for that target. The mature endeavor is our "there." Pray about it—Spirit-inspired visons are the key to our success. Then do your research and write down as many details as you can.

For example, the bull's eye of our Real Life marketplace church is developing thriving multiple cities in the U.S. and abroad by developing their entrepreneurs. What is your dream of the marketplace in your city?

When my team and I envisioned what God was inspiring us toward, we saw a multisite church embedded in the economy, translating the gospel for the unchurched, and equipping whole-life disciples to expand God's Kingdom and its presence in the marketplace. But we could never get there if we didn't chart the path to it.

- **Chart a path**

The path connects our "here" to our "there." It is helpful if the path is penned on paper. Our brains process and retain well visual maps.

Because we've already defined our "there," we need to realistically assess the present situation of our "here" in order to envision what road to take and what steps to put in place.

- **Define obtainable and measurable first steps**

Your first steps are important. You usually have several preparatory steps to take to position you for a successful transition from where you are to get on the road heading to there.

Be realistic about your time and resources as you chart the steps and give yourself and your church obtainable timelines to achieve them. Otherwise, you'll get discouraged fast and may be likely to decide that becoming a marketplace-embedded church wasn't a good idea.

- **Define obtainable and measurable next steps**

Your next steps keep the momentum going. Unfortunately, after the initial steps, many entrepreneurs run out of steam and their endeavors crash, because the excitement of the newness wears off and all that's left is hard work. Birthing a new venture is a costly endeavor—it will require resources, energy, commitment, and focus, but the results and the Master's reward are well worth it.

I'm sure that to bury our one talent might seem like less work in the moment, but it's disastrous in the long run. You have to keep taking Holy Spirit–inspired action and measure the success of each step by evaluating whether the goals that you set for that step were accomplished. We are called to faithfully steward the treasures of King Jesus. Let's not tire of being fruitful.

Our Real Life dream of thriving multiple cities will involve equipping multiple church planters to start marketplace churches in multiple U.S. locations and around the globe. This is a lofty vision. Many of us will be overwhelmed by the magnitude of a vision that either hasn't taken its first breath or is in its infancy stage.

The key to success, without letting our heads spin, is to envision steps appropriate to our maturity stage. When going after your endeavor, don't compare your beginning with someone else's middle or end.

For example, we desire to involve all of our 3 B's—bodies, buildings, and bucks—to grow the entrepreneurs in our city but, for now, our capacity only allows us to support them with two of the 3 B's. With the first B—bodies—Real Life personnel and volunteers are leading entrepreneurial programs, workshops, trainings, and networking events.

With the second B—buildings—we are offering private offices and common co-working space. We haven't built enough capacity for our third B—bucks—to have investment capital for entrepreneurial startups. We are learning to be patient and pace our compassion to match our capacity and find joy even in the limitations we experience as we expand the Kingdom of God in our city among the entrepreneurs we serve.

> Envisioning the future is only as good as your desire to take divinely inspired action toward that future.

It is important to remember envisioning the future is only as good as your desire to take divinely inspired action toward that future. Leaders must sometimes be willing to become unpopular until their model is proven, boldly taking risks as they put structures and systems in place to ensure the success of their venture.

Why Do We Need to Measure?

We need to know if the church is doing its job. One day the Master will measure His ROI (return on investment) (Matthew

25). We had better measure along the way to assure that we are found faithful.

How Do We Measure It?

We are convinced we must measure, but how will we measure the church's success? Do we measure in numbers or some intangibles that are hard to define? Are numbers good, constricting, or bad? There is nothing inherently bad in numbers, whether it comes to people, money, or buildings. The critical point is what we measure.

Admittedly, there is a difference between measuring quantity versus quality. Quality means different things to different people. It's sometimes hard, but it's possible to measure both.

If you are measuring spiritual maturity, it helps if the pastors establish a baseline for what they consider a disciple to be and then measure those characteristics as evident in the lives of the congregants.

For example, we can measure conversions, water baptisms, the number of people becoming whole-life disciples, and those brought off drugs. We can also measure economic impact by counting the number of entrepreneurs helped to start a new business or academic scholarships for business education.

Measuring kids brought off the street or helped to improve in school, those sent to an entrepreneurial program, or teens given scholarships for summer camp shows the way the church impacts the life of the next generation. Although it's hard to measure social capital, we can still measure the community projects the church gets involved in, the civic organizations it engages, and the relationships the congregants establish with people from the community.

We can measure homeless people housed, or unemployed people trained for jobs. Whatever your church is focused on, you can measure the impact you are making in your community and on the marketplace. The numbers you count give you an opportunity to celebrate the way your church grows, supports your community, and advances the Kingdom of God.

Bodies. Churches for Monday count the people they reach in the Sunday-to-Monday Bridge, not only the Sunday worship event. We can count the unemployed we train for work, the entrepreneurs we convene for a meetup, the singles gathering at our facility for coffee, and the kids' play dates our daycares offer to the community. There are many opportunities to impact people in the marketplace, and we can measure the lives we touch by counting bodies.

Bucks. Churches for Monday count the budget of the church. However, they also count the economic development they cause for the local economy and beyond, as well as the upward economic lift they facilitate for the congregants and people from the community. Churches can help develop or scale business by training the business owners or investing in the business. They can add to the workforce by providing job training or job retraining, and they can add economic value by supporting young people with academic or training scholarships.

Buildings. Buildings are great assets to the church and can become a valuable asset to the community. Churches for Monday count how many ways the buildings are used to create touches with the community and provide vital, meaningful resources to further education, work, and play.

For example, empty Sunday school classrooms can be used to house entrepreneurs looking for an office space during the week. The fellowship halls can be rented out for community events, birthday parties, bridal showers, or business trainings. The gymnasiums can bring sports to the community's youth who may otherwise never come to church on Sunday. The church yards can be used for photography sessions by budding photographers or by moms with kids for play dates. Having people experience your facility outside of Sunday makes it likely they may visit your church in the future.

We can label the 3 B's as passé and not spiritual enough, and we may want to throw them away. Still, we cannot escape the fact that any earthly enterprise operates on bodies, budgets, and buildings (or virtual spaces).

We can pretend we are not going to count the 3 B's—but we all know we will. We have to. Otherwise, one Sunday we might be meeting on the sidewalk because someone did not account for the right budget.

The pressing question is not, "Do we discard the scorecard?" but, "Can we thoughtfully revamp it for greater Kingdom impact, which counts both the Sunday worship and the Monday mission?"

A Movement

Churches preparing for Monday are on the rise and are becoming a movement. They equip whole-life disciples on Sunday for mission at work on Monday. They guide believers on how to effectively translate the gospel for their postmodern friends to hear.

If you are someone who has not engaged the 8-to-5 window for impact, but are curious about it, this is an invitation to reenter the mission of God with renewed fervor to see you and others transform.

Questions for Reflection and Application

1. Pastor, how can you bring an entrepreneurial spirit to the way you conduct ministry and outreach, but, like the Papazovs, keep the essentials of the gospel, the church, and the Kingdom central?

2. Real Life Church hosted an actual business incubator as an outreach to their community. Brainstorm some ways that your church could bridge the Sunday-to-Monday gap and incubate people in their workplace assignments?

3. Dr. Papazov uses scripture to challenge the *de facto* church scorecard, and challenges us to move toward a more Kingdom-centric scorecard. How can you move toward a more biblical way of measuring the win for your congregation?

Dr. Rev. Svetlana Papazov is a wife, mother of two, lead pastor of Real Life Church, seminary professor, church consultant, and business coach. As a professional member of the National Speakers Association, she presents at conferences and retreats, and she trains and consults with various denominational networks, associations, churches, and marketplace leaders to become change catalysts for their communities.

Svetlana has been featured in and has written for well-known publications and magazines such as *Barna: The State of Pastors*, *Influence* magazine, *Evangel*, *Leading Hearts*, and more. She is also the author of the breakthrough book *Church for Monday: Equipping Believers for Mission at Work*, which equips believers to close the Sunday-to-Monday gap to flourish communities spiritually, socially, and economically.

Church for Monday offers a fresh, outside-the-box, entrepreneurial paradigm for ministry. It guides the local church to retool in order to prepare believers for the work week on Monday, regain relevance in the lives of the lapsed and non-Christians, and reestablish the Church's witness in the public arena. This is the gospel for a new generation and the how-to churches have been looking for. *Church for Monday* is an essential read for anyone who longs to see the Good News reach beyond Sunday into a waiting, seven-day-a-week world.

To connect with or book Dr. Svetlana Papazov for your next event, please visit ChurchForMonday.com or email svetlana@rlcrva.com.

6

Equipping Christians to Advance God's Kingdom in and Through Business

John E. Mulford

The church today is anemic, in part because it does not fully embrace its biblical mission. Local churches are either inward-focused or focused on a small subset of the ways God has commanded them to take the gospel to the world.

The mission of the church is to extend God's Kingdom by imaging Jesus Christ. It does this by:

- Teaching and training people throughout the world in God's ways (Matthew 28:19)
- Being salt and light (Matthew 5:13–16)
- Demonstrating God's love (John 13:34–35)

What is the church doing to reach the world? Evangelism, mission trips, Bible translation, feeding the poor, etc. These are all laudable, but they omit valuable tools in God's toolkit, and they involve only a small fraction of believers in churches. The church needs to engage all its members with its mission and expand its reach into the marketplace.

God wants all His children to serve Him 24/7, consciously advancing His agenda every day in all their activities. These activities include interacting with family, neighbors, church members, and people in the marketplace. The marketplace represents one of the largest, if not *the* largest, investments of an adult's time in the 21st century.

The marketplace should receive high priority in the church, but it doesn't because of an incomplete or distorted biblical worldview. Take the example of how many churches do evangelism.

Today's evangelism often looks like raids from a fort (church) into enemy territory to rescue prisoners and bring them back to the fort for safety. Sound overstated?

> God will redeem His whole creation—both people and the earth

Consider that most evangelism consists of church members inviting people they know to come to church, where the pastor is expected to convince the visitors to believe the gospel and join the church. Or, if the church is bold, it sends teams to confront strangers on the streets with the truth of the gospel, hoping that some will believe and begin attending church.

This model of evangelism reveals an underlying worldview with several unbiblical elements: the world is evil, the world is controlled by Satan, and God wants to rescue people from the evil world before He destroys it. It is no surprise that people operating with this worldview are afraid of the world, see no future in investing in it, and want to rescue others from the world to join them in the safety of the church.

Each of these views is a distortion of biblical truth. After the Fall, every person was born a sinner, but God never called His creation evil. Satan exerts much power in the world, but he is no match for God. God will redeem His whole creation—both people and the earth.

Let's look at a biblical worldview, especially as it concerns activities outside the walls of the church. God created man in

His image to have relationship with Him. Man is not just a spiritual being, but also a physical one. God gave man dominion over the earth and everything in it, to develop it and steward it to the Glory of the Creator. This is the Dominion-Stewardship (D-S) mandate.

Work is the vehicle for accomplishing the D-S mandate and is essential to each worker's identity. We are created in the image of Creator God, who is a worker Himself. After the Fall, work became more difficult, but no less essential to both man's survival and his fulfillment.

Work serves many roles in God's D-S mandate and redemptive plan. Work provides:

- An important way for man to have relationship with God and with his fellow man.
- Fulfillment of man's created purpose (Ecclesiastes 5:12).
- A vehicle for learning character—God uses work relationships to teach many biblical values, such as excellence, humility, generosity, forgiveness, honesty, and so on.
- The means for supplying our own needs and those of our families.
- The means for producing surplus, which we can give to others in need (Ephesians 4:28).
- The means by which we implement scientific discoveries. Because He is the God of order, we can have faith that we will discover how the universe

operates and develop productive technology based on these scientific laws.

- The means by which we steward and care for the earth. We develop the earth through economic activity. Abundance makes it easier for us to take care of God's creation. If you don't believe that, compare the environmental quality and safety in low-income versus high-income nations.

In today's modern economy, few people work alone. They are part of organizations. They interact with people both inside and outside their organizations.

Large, complex organizations are microcosms of the world, Petri dishes for man's relationship with man. If the business is worldly, then worldly, sinful ways are reinforced. If the business is godly, then God's ways can be taught and reinforced.

God has a plan to redeem His whole creation—both man and the earth (Romans 8:19–23; Ephesians 1:7; Revelation 5:9). Business is central to that plan because it is the vehicle for developing the earth, and it is where people spend most of their time. Where better to meet God than at work, through the love and godly actions of believers in business?

Godly business will convey honesty, integrity, care, compassion, kindness, sacrifice, steadfastness, repentance, forgiveness, faith, and trust. As you exhibit these behaviors and truths, people will want to do business with you. Broken, hurting employees, customers, and even strangers will seek you out to receive your love and answers to their problems.

So, business is key to advancing God's Kingdom on earth—that is, developing the earth to yield its bounty, stewarding God's earth, and transmitting God's love and truth through business relationships and transactions. Kingdom business leaders have the privilege of leading God's transformation of people and nations into the image of Jesus Christ (2 Corinthians 3:18).

The idea that the church should be involved in the marketplace is not new. But as with many issues, the church's understanding has fluctuated over history. There have been cycles of engagement followed by disengagement, influenced significantly by the dominant worldview in the church during each cycle.

The social gospel movement of the late 19th and early 20th centuries was a reaction to the urban problems of industrialization. The question "What Would Jesus Do?" from Charles Sheldon's book *In His Steps* describes the movement. Activists sought to repair damage they perceived was caused by unbridled capitalism. They were providing a "cup of water to the thirsty," but not transforming the workplace into what God intended in His Dominion-Stewardship Mandate.

During most of the 20th century, a premillennial view became prominent in many protestant churches. Lively debates on eschatology among theologians affected the worldview taught in churches. Popular books like *The Late Great Planet Earth* and the *Left Behind* series reinforced the premillennial, pretribulation view many heard in church. That view led many Christians to act according to the "lifeboat" metaphor—rescue people from the sinking ship of earth, but don't waste time investing in it.

The lifeboat metaphor influenced many of my MBA students in the 1980s. The metaphor shaped their beliefs about the concepts of "full-time ministry" and "sacred versus secular," which affected their attitudes toward business.

How many times have you heard a believer say, "I envy them because they are in full-time ministry"? This brief statement conveys a belief that people with "ministry" occupations serve God all the time, while others only serve God during their part-time church activities.

> No Christian is assigned part-time service.

Those same believers think of ministry as sacred work of eternal value, but business as secular work of limited, temporal importance. Pastors often perpetuate this thinking by indicating that their calling as pastor is somehow higher or more valuable to God than other callings.

During the 1980s, my MBA students who expressed these views felt guilty about their calling to business rather than "ministry." When I investigated, I discovered that their feelings derived from churches teaching that the sacred jobs of pastor or missionary were more valuable to God than secular jobs in business.

I told the students that if they believed in Jesus Christ as their Savior and Lord, they were in full-time, 24/7 Christian service, whether they recognized it or not. No Christian is assigned part-time service. It was hard to overcome years of exposure to the pessimistic view of business with a few lectures.

This misunderstanding about "ministry" can lead to unwise decisions. Take, for example, my friend wanting to sell his company so he could go into full-time ministry as a missionary.

I challenged him: "You want to make disciples in a country where the language and culture are foreign to you. How long will it take you to learn to communicate and gain credibility so that people will listen to you? Why do you want to relinquish your role as leader of a company of 500 employees who already respect you and want your guidance in their lives?"

He didn't see running a 500-person firm as a calling or ministry. That was the attitude of most Christian executives and business owners I knew in the 1980s.

Because the churches were not ministering to businesspeople and helping them understand and thrive in their calling to business, nonprofit organizations filled the gap. Early efforts, such as Christian Business Men's Committee (CBMC), founded in 1930 in Chicago, and Full Gospel Business Men's Fellowship International (FGBMFI), founded in 1951 in Los Angeles, focused on evangelizing and ministering to people in the marketplace. That is, winning people to Christ and helping them live the Christian life, whether at home or at work.

Organizations founded in the 1970s, '80s, and '90s focused on business owners, because owners had the power to shape the culture of their organizations. The Fellowship of Companies for Christ International (FCCI), founded in Atlanta in 1977, the International Christian Chamber of Commerce (ICCC), founded in Sweden in the early 1980s, and The C12 Group, founded in Tampa, Florida, in 1992, shared not only an interest in business owners, but also in equipping them with biblical principles to help them run their businesses for Christ.

As Dean of a business school, I was very interested in this phenomenon. I talked with many members of these organizations, attended their meetings, served on the boards of two

(FCCI and C12), and partnered with a third (ICCC) to launch a business development center in Rwanda. The most common concerns I heard, distilled from discussions with many members, were:

- My pastor doesn't understand me. He doesn't appreciate my needs and what I have to offer the church.
- I'm mainly viewed as an ATM for the church.
- The opportunities I have at church, such as usher or carpenter on a mission trip, don't utilize my business knowledge and leadership skills.

These businesspeople found a home in parachurch business organizations. They shared common experiences and skills and received encouragement about using their business success as a "platform for ministry." That is, people would listen to their testimony because of their business success.

For about ten years, I challenged my friends in this movement to modify the concept, changing it to "business *as* ministry" rather than "business as a platform for ministry." To me, a platform indicated a place above others from which the person in authority disseminated his wisdom.

This may have a place for people outside the organization. The organization's success attracts them to listen to a message of godly wisdom and truth. However, members of the organization are family. Family members minister to each other best out of love, not out of a position of authority or financial success.

In the early 1990s, I was impressed with the way an insurance company had implemented *Business As Ministry*. The owner not only treated employees as family, but their families were also considered part of the company family. He ministered to his "family" as a loving father.

When an employee, who was doing an excellent job for his company, felt a calling to a career outside the company, he not only released the employee to pursue that calling, but also invested in that person's future. He viewed the employee as a whole person, not just a productive asset. He also invested in his employees' children because they were also part of the company family.

To achieve Kingdom impact, the owner knew he needed to counter Satan's attacks with intercessory prayer. The qualifications for an intercessor were a heart for God and an attentive spirit, not an advanced degree or business skills. Many prayers were answered.

God ministered in and through this insurance company to employees, their families, customers, and the community. Many broken relationships were healed, and many came to the Lord. *Business As Ministry* is now practiced in many companies, but it is far from the norm, even among companies owned by Christians.

The movement that was started by parachurch business organizations expanded as the concepts of Business as Ministry were promoted through books, conferences, websites, podcasts, and so on. Christian businesspeople were mobilized. Churches had to play catch-up, which some did better than others.

Some of the business owners and executives who had flocked to parachurch organizations because they weren't being fed at church are now leading business groups in their churches. Some pastors observed the movement and embraced it. Others felt the movement threatened their theology, their control, or both. The following example illustrates the challenge.

I worked with an organization that recruited business executives from churches to participate in executive education in developing nations. The organization's CEO tried to recruit business executives by first meeting with pastors to get their buy-in.

Most pastors either dismissed the idea or argued against it. The pastors didn't want to share their key business leaders with a parachurch organization that would divert the time and resources of the business leaders away from the church.

The CEO tried meeting with mission pastors. They liked the international aspect but couldn't grasp the power of sending businesspeople who lacked missions training. He achieved the most success when he captured the attention and interest of a strong business leader in a church. Those leaders had credibility and trust with pastors, staff, and businesspeople in the church. They became champions for his program.

The multifaceted movement I have briefly described above has had a dramatic effect on student attitudes toward business. Feelings of guilt about a calling to the marketplace have slowly been replaced by excitement.

Many popular books have affirmed the calling to work (such as Doug Sherman's *Your Work Matters to God* and Timothy Keller's *Every Good Endeavor*) and the role of business in God's plan (for example, Ken Eldred's *God Is at Work* and Ed Silvoso's *Anointed for Business*). Now divinity students envy business students because the latter are called to where the "action is." Some pastors seem to envy businesspeople for their natural access to people who won't come to church.

While much progress has been made, much remains to be done. Many businesspeople are ahead of churches in their thinking about advancing the Kingdom in the marketplace. However, others, for whom Business As Ministry is a new concept, are disadvantaged by a lack of church understanding and encouragement.

> Pastors focus on the 10% because evangelicals are giving a median of 1%. But God owns 100%.

Sometimes a pastor can address a legitimate concern but unintentionally undermine the Dominion-Stewardship worldview. Tithing is a good example. To fund the church and encourage members to enjoy the satisfaction that comes from giving, many pastors say something like this: "Please consider giving a tithe. That is only 10% of your income. You get to keep the other 90%."

They focus on the 10% because evangelicals are giving only a median of 1%. But God owns 100%. We have a stewardship responsibility to God for how we use every resource He puts in our hands. By giving us "permission" to use 90% of our income as we want, pastors are causing the congregation to take their eyes off how to steward all their resources to advance God's Kingdom throughout the earth.

Even when a church preaches Dominion-Stewardship clearly, it often fails in its implementation. Preaching is only part of the job. The church is called to equip saints for works of service. Equipping requires more than preaching. It also means teaching, training, action learning and practice, mentoring, feedback, coaching, and so on.

Many churches have onboarding programs that welcome newcomers to the church. They consist of, "This is what we believe; this is how we are structured, and this is what we expect of you as members." Upon completion, everyone is asked to volunteer for a "job" in the church, such as usher, nursery worker, Sunday school teacher, cook, intercessor, and so on.

These are all good, but it is like a CEO telling employees to choose an area that will maintain the internal workings of the business, such as building maintenance, events for employee morale, and the benefits or benevolence committee. These are necessary, but they are like chores at home. Everyone must shoulder part of the work, but their chores do not define them, nor should they be their primary activity.

The purpose of business is to make and deliver life-improving products and services to customers. The purpose of the church is to advance God's Kingdom by imaging Christ in the world.

Business gets outside its walls when it interacts with customers, suppliers, the government, and so on. The church gets outside its walls when it encourages its members to serve God 24/7 wherever they are.

One major role of pastors and church leaders is to equip the body of Christ for these works of service (Ephesians 4:11–12). Here are some suggestions for a comprehensive equipping approach:

- Establish your equipping program guided by the mission and vision of the church. The following mission statement provides a good launch point for an equipping program.

> *We are a community called to image Jesus Christ in His renewing of all things. We image Jesus Christ in this renewal by loving God and loving others—i.e., worshipping God, developing followers of Jesus, cultivating community, engaging in evangelism, transforming culture, and caring for creation.* (Westminster Reformed Presbyterian Church, Suffolk, Virginia).

- Provide Scriptural foundation and framework from the pulpit.
- Challenge all church members to discover and pursue their life purpose and calling.
- Provide teaching and training to equip everyone in their calling.
- Provide an environment for people to practice their calling, receive encouragement, and testify about what God is doing in and through them.

One last suggestion to churches that are serious about equipping the saints to advance God's Kingdom in and through business. Don't sugarcoat the challenge. Today's business environment is hostile to many biblical values and to those who openly espouse them.

Send them out with the words of Jesus: "Behold, I am sending you out as sheep in the midst of wolves, so be wise as serpents and innocent as doves." (Matthew 10:16 ESV)

Questions for Reflection and Application

1. The author points out the strategic importance of the marketplace to the Great Commission, but that the Church's worldview has kept her from placing appropriate priority on the marketplace. How much of a priority is it receiving in your church?

2. Dr. Mulford suggests that churches should help people discover their life purpose and calling, and to equip them in this calling. Do you have a systematic way to do this as part of your equipping and discipleship ministry?

Dr. John Mulford joined Regent University as a founding faculty member in the Business School in 1982. In addition to serving as a professor, he has served as Dean of the Business School, Chief Financial Officer and Chief Investment Officer of Regent University, as well as founder and director of Regent Center for Entrepreneurship.

Through the Center, he has pursued his passion for helping entrepreneurs start and grow businesses in dozens of countries, most notably by creating with colleague Jason Benedict a model for Business Development Centers that has been licensed in nine countries.

Prior to his time at Regent, John conducted policy research at the Rand Corporation and served as Vice President and Senior Economist at First Interstate Bank of California. He earned his B.S. in Engineering, Magna Cum Laude, from Brown University, and a Ph.D. in

Regional Economics from Cornell University, where he was a National Science Foundation Fellow.

7
Citywide Workplace Network
Chuck Proudfit

I grew up believing that all you had to do to be happy was study hard, get into a good university, get a good job with a good organization, make a stable income, and retire comfortably. Well, as painful as it is now to write those words, that's what I originally set out to do with my young adult life.

I studied hard, got into Harvard University, and landed an executive job making a very good salary working for the world's largest consumer products company. According to the "formula" I "caught" in the culture growing up, I should have been very happy indeed—but I wasn't. I felt completely empty.

My life was devoid of a deeper meaning, and the place where it emerged the most was in my everyday work. I was spending most of my waking hours at work, yet I was toiling at tasks with little long-term significance for me. My frustration with work led to a spiritual search.

Over the course of a decade, I studied the original source material of all the major world religions and philosophies. I gradually came to believe that following Jesus Christ is the only way to fulfillment—in work and in all of life. I came to a saving faith as a young, thirtysomething working professional. Frustration with work had led me to faith, and now I started sensing the urgency to bring faith into my work.

At Work on Purpose (www.atworkonpurpose.org) has become the culmination of that urgency. It is a citywide workplace ministry community engaging over 12,000 people in Cincinnati, Ohio, but our growth emerged from humble beginnings. Before we launched the ministry back in 2003, I was already fortunate to be the founder of a business consultancy, affording me extensive opportunities to experiment with faith expression at work.

> Christians are eager to explore the premise of faith at work, if it is presented in a practical and actionable way.

While my journey was certainly filled with trial and error—and clashed with the culture's expectation that work is a secular endeavor—I gradually learned how to be "faith-active" at work. I discovered that Christian faith contributes significantly to vocational flourishing, and I sensed a nudge from the Lord to guide other working Christians toward the same. My initial concept was simple but sound—a small group for "work life."

I handpicked about a dozen working Christians from different local churches, denominations, and locations across the city. We met twice a month on a weeknight, with free-flowing conversations about applying a Christian worldview to the myriad challenges and opportunities affecting all of us at work.

The Holy Spirit was thick in our midst, and these conversations were *electric*. Entirely through word of mouth, with no organized curriculum, no sponsoring ministry, and no budget funding, we grew to over 300 participants within six months!

I came to realize that Christians are eager to explore the premise of faith at work, as long as it is presented in a practical and actionable way. Globally, about 97% of working Christians are employed outside of the local church or parachurch, so we must speak to their needs in the context of private, public, and social sector employment.

Working Christians represent a vast resource for redemptive work in our world. God has deployed us strategically across every channel of cultural influence, so we are positioned for significant potential Kingdom impact.

Almost every city has a variety of workplace ministries, but few cities have a connected network of workplace ministries, local churches engaged in workplace ministry, and faith-active workplace Christians at large. Cincinnati is blessed to have such a network.

Over the years, we have realized that At Work on Purpose has four differentiating characteristics framing our expression of citywide workplace ministry. First, we have a city vision, that a day would come when every working Christian in Greater Cincinnati would be faith-active at work.

Second, we are ecumenical in posture within the Christian tradition, cutting across church homes, denominations, zip codes, and ministries.

Third, we are organized as a network rather than a traditional parachurch organization.

Fourth, we emphasize cultural as well as vocational flourishing, so that we pursue the peace and prosperity of the cities where we work and live.

One of the exciting aspects of our network model is that ideas and initiatives flow freely across the city. For example, we are cultivating faith-based entrepreneurship in and through the local church. We have launched a "community of practice" for about a half-dozen Greater Cincinnati local churches pursuing entrepreneurial ventures within their facilities, and we are now extending this community for national reach and impact. We are also discipling Christian workplace leaders through innovative small groups called "collaboratories." These are "collaborative laboratories" guiding Christian workplace leaders not just to steward organizations, but also to serve all people in their spheres of influence, shape industries by establish benchmarks for operational excellence, and serve communities by engaging philanthropically.

> For all working Christians, we provide a foundational equipping experience called Mission2Monday.

In addition, we have marketplace ministries providing pathways for citizens returning from incarceration to find gainful employment, which we match to whole-life discipleship for sustainable success as contributing citizens.

For all working Christians, we provide a foundational equipping experience called Mission2Monday. The premise is that work is one of our most strategic mission fields for the Lord, and that we build our witness at work one wise choice at a time. Time and again, it's the tough choices at work that make all the difference in how we present ourselves as "salt and light."

In simple terms, we need to choose to: integrate faith into every aspect of our work; respond to God's vocational call for us; commit to Kingdom standards of conduct at work; serve others through everyday work; and steward the resources of the work world for a hurting world around us.

I get excited when I see just one working Christian pursuing work like this, but *dream with me* ... imagine the spiritual power of hundreds or thousands of working Christians looking like this across a city's workplace!

In the marketplace, story branding is a method for communicating a concept where the customer is the "hero" of an adventure, and the product or service provider is the "guide" along the way. I have found that our hero is the "faithful working Christian" who diligently pursues the adventure of "vocational fulfillment."

At Work on Purpose guides working Christians to discover purposeful employment, experience vocational discipleship, and contribute workplace engagement. The villain in the adventure is "secularized work."

Through an annual conference called XL, we celebrate the stories of working Christians who find and fulfill their highest and best use at work; who equip themselves and others for full faith expression at work; and who serve the workplace spiritually through their jobs, in the organizations, and for their industries and communities. As time has passed, we have discovered a helpful way to best organize our efforts across the city. It was inspired by Stanley McChrystal's book *Team of Teams*.

Deployed by then-President George W. Bush to combat Al-Qaeda in Iraq, McChrystal quickly discovered that the "shock and awe" military of the United States was being out-maneuvered by a decentralized, organic, and highly adaptive set of interconnected terrorist cells.

To become competitive, McChrystal restricted the U.S. military in Iraq with a similar "team of teams" organizational structure. Here, functional teams were defined and deployed with high levels of autonomy and authority to move effectively in an environment with a rapid pace of change as well as complex conditions on the ground.

> Our Movement teams address Kingdom enterprises, city transformation, and citywide models.

For At Work on Purpose, our team-based infrastructure starts with the Mission teams addressing purposeful employment, vocational discipleship, and workplace engagement. Our Ministry teams address prayer coverage, community events, and equipping tools. Our Management teams address strategic direction, administrative operations, and financial stewardship.

Our Movement teams address Kingdom enterprises, city transformation, and citywide models. We also have an Executive Team that "travels" across these teams to ensure that they are connected and collaborating well together. This is a network model for organizing and is quite different than the more traditional organizational structures for local churches and parachurches.

As we explore supporting other cities to develop similar models, we are learning some important insights. First, each citywide workplace ministry needs a catalyzing leader who can convene, inspire, and organize working Christians into a decentralized and organic network of spiritual influence across a city.

Second, the mix of participating workplace ministries, local churches, parachurches, and working Christians is unique to the context of each city.

Third, the most foundational "unit of scale" is the faithful working Christian who successfully advances through purposeful employment, vocational discipleship, and workplace engagement. We are early in this journey of scalability and welcome the opportunity to interact with any of you who should read this and have further interest.

Questions for Reflection and Application

1. Based on the example of the citywide workplace movement in Cincinnati, what are some ways that you could help initiate or support such an effort in your community? Jot down two or three actionable items.

2. What are some of the advantages of a citywide network over a typical marketplace ministry parachurch organization?

3. What role does the local church play in a citywide workplace ministry network?

Chuck Proudfit began following Christ in 1997. He was seeking practical ways to live out Christian faith at work, and quickly discovered just how hard it is. The marketplace didn't like to talk about "religion and politics," and the local church was largely disengaged from the tough spiritual realities of modern work life.

Applying his research background from Harvard University, Chuck spent several years studying how Christians live out faith at work and how scripture speaks to our experiences. He uncovered a consistent set of spiritual struggles faced by all working Christians, as well as a compelling set of spiritual solutions drawn straight from God's Word.

These insights formed the framework for At Work on Purpose, launched in 2003. Its community now includes over 12,000 working Christians across Greater Cincinnati, and it has become one of the nation's leading prototypes for citywide workplace ministry. Chuck is also the Founder and President of SKILLSOURCE,® a consultancy employing over thirty contractors and delivering sustainable client growth through applied Biblical principles.

Chuck developed his general management expertise at three industry-leading firms: The Procter & Gamble Company, The Ernest & Julio Gallo Winery, and LensCrafters Corporation. At Harvard University, he pioneered the school's organizational development curriculum. An avid educator, Chuck has served as an adjunct faculty member at the Great Oaks Institute and Cincinnati Christian University.

Chuck has received the Angel Award for community service from the Smith Family Foundation, and the Best Award from Nehemiah Foundation. He has led SKILLSOURCE® to a Tri-State Success Award for exceptional business growth, a Torch Award ethics commendation from the Better Business Bureau, a Perfect 10 Certified Corporate Culture designation, and a C-Suite recognition from LEAD.

Chuck advises a wide range of national and international ministries, including Transform Our World, the Great Awakening Project, GoodCities, Nuway Foundation, Self-Sustaining Enterprises, and Declare. Chuck is also an Elder at Grace Chapel.

Chuck is the co-author of *BIZNISTRY: Transforming Lives through Enterprise*, and the author of *Citywide Workplace Ministry in a Box*. Chuck holds a Black Belt in Tae Kwon Do under U.S. Olympic Coach Hong Kong Kim. He and his wife, Jeryl, have two children, Aidan and Maya, both adopted from South Korea.

8
Do You Want to Pastor or Transform Your City?

David Robinson

I guess the questions must be asked: Do you want to pastor your city, or do you want to transform your city? Do you want to provide for the shepherding needs of your city, or do you want to transform the marketplace where all spiritual battles for dominate influence are won or lost? Are you providing sheep who are healthy and well-fed, or are you training Kingdom Warriors who are possessing the gates (places of influence) in your city?

How you answer these questions will not only determine your passion for what's to come in this chapter, but also the ministry strategy with which you approach the battle between the Kingdom of Light and the kingdom of darkness for control of your city.

If you have the title, position, gifting, and function of pastor, you have a wonderful gift that is critical to the people of God. As it was in Jesus's day, the masses are hurting and wandering about, as scripture says, sheep without a shepherd. The Church cannot create an army of warriors out of wounded, broken, and hurting people.

To report for duty on the front lines of spiritual warfare, you must be reasonably healthy and able to stand the rigors of training and development. That is the role of the pastor/shepherd along with the teacher. This role cannot be discounted in any way. The health of God's army must come before any level of effective warfare can be waged, much less victories won.

The first gift a new Christian must meet is that of pastor. It's the pastor who meets them at the altar of sin sacrifice that helps them get healed from sin and the effects of a sinful lifestyle. However, to become a warrior that can take on the enemy of Christ and the Church requires the input of the other four Ephesians 4 gifts.

> The purpose of salvation and Holy Spirit baptism was to transform the marketplace, the place where most lost people go every day.

Only the full expression of Christ can win the victory in the day of battle. The role of church leadership is to equip the saints for the ministry. Church work is what goes on inside our facilities and at our gatherings. The work of the Church is what happens in the public square, the marketplace.

For the Church to have prophetic marketplace influence and effectively address the biblical purpose for God's people in Genesis 22:17 and 24:60, as well as the assigned mission in Matthew 28:18–20, she must embrace the priesthood of all Believers, not a small select group.

The purpose of Jesus's coming was to destroy the works of the devil, the evil one. Though he does act up at times in Church, his main activity takes place in the marketplace.

The purpose of salvation and Holy Spirit baptism was to transform the marketplace, the place where most lost people go every day. The coming of Jesus to the earth, followed by the

Holy Spirit on the Day of Pentecost, was not to swell the church roles, but to win lost souls and transform cities and nations.

The Bible says in Psalm 2:8 (NJKV), "Ask of Me, and I will give You the nations for Your inheritance." This was the precursor to the command in Matthew to disciple all nations. I can assure you; those nations don't come easy and require a lot of resources.

Winning the lost and turning them into frontline warriors requires more than the pastoral gift. It requires the full complement of Christ's gifts in Ephesians 4 with a clear understanding of God's purpose for His people: "your descendants shall possess the gate of their enemies" (Genesis 22:17 NKJV). You cannot disciple a nation until you possess the places of influence.

Until bold, confident marketplace ministers infiltrate the "gates of influence" that control every city, state, and nation, they remain the stronghold of the enemy. The business gate pays for everything. The government gate controls everything through laws and regulations. The educational gate determines the values, philosophy, and worldview that business and government leaders use every day to make determinations.

Our marketplace ministers must not only infiltrate these gates of influence, but they must also allow God's favor to elevate them through the value they bring to their ministry assignment and rise to the level of dominant influence. Once in this place of influence, they model Christian values and lead every day as Jesus would.

Church leader, you must train your marketplace leaders not to be a PAC, political action committee, influencing these gates of influence as an activist promoting some type of Liberation

Theology. God has not called the Church to change its marketplace culture through pressure, endorsements, or public displays. None of which are necessarily wrong—it's just not God's assignment for the Church. Our mission as Christians is being salt and light while gathering the harvest of future harvesters.

Possessing the Gates of the Enemy

> That in blessing I will bless thee, and in multiplying I will multiply thy seed as the stars of the heaven, and as the sand which is upon the sea shore; and thy seed shall possess the gate of his enemies; (Genesis 22:17 KJV)

> And they blessed Rebekah and said to her: "Our sister, may you become The mother of thousands of ten thousands; And may your descendants possess The gates of those who hate them." (Genesis 24:60 NKJV)

It seems that leadership is suffering from moral spiritual autoimmune deficiency, the integrity to resist sin is gone. Regardless of your eschatology, every generation must confront evil in the marketplace of their day.

The Gospel not only has the power to save people from sin, but also to empower them to change the culture and possess the places of influence, leading to the discipling of entire nations. Without intentionally, neither will happen.

Without Church leaders training their people to not only be servants within their spiritual family, but also frontline Kingdom Warriors running toward and defeating the Goliaths of their day. Historically, it seems that God's people surrender too often and too willingly their God-given rightful place of authority and influence, the power of Tsaddiguim, the Hebrew word for righteous.

When righteous people are in power, the Bible says the people rejoice. When evil people are in power, the people mourn. Scripturally, there is no question that God wants righteous people to be in places of authority and possess the gates of influence.

The gates of the Old Testament cities were places of influence. Issues of mercy, judgment, righteousness, education, and business were discussed and decided by the elders in the gates.

Today, the righteous are not only not welcome in places of influence and authority, but they are also mocked and disdained. There was a time in America when the Judeo-Christian ethic and morality ruled, but no longer. It seems that Isaiah's prophecy has come true:

> Our courts oppose the righteous man; fairness is unknown. Truth falls dead in the streets, and justice is outlawed. (Isaiah 59:14 TLB)

When the New Testament writers were looking for a word to describe first-century believers, they chose the word *ecclesia*, the called-out ones. Other words were available, but they chose from the Septuagint, the Old Testament translated into Greek. The assembly of the righteous in the Old Testament is now the assembled church in the New Testament marketplace.

The Body of Christ is most scattered on Sundays when it meets in its local congregations. It is most gathered on Mondays when they minister in the marketplace. Church leader/pastor, you must prepare them for both places.

For its first 150 years, it was the Church that held the places of influences in America—business, government, and education—but no long-er. To prove it, you have to look no further than the laws that were passed to remove prayer and Bible reading from the classrooms, the re-writing of school textbooks, and open support of sinful lifestyles.

> Any ability or talent first comes from God before it can be developed into a strength.

What are the places of influence, the controlling gates God promised Abraham and his seed, that you and I would possess? First, the business gate. According to Deuteronomy 8:18, it's the Lord our God who gives the power to create wealth.

Any ability or talent first comes from God before it can be developed into a strength. There are people, sinners, who have a gift for which they give God no credit. However, it does not diminish their gift to create wealth.

As believers, we know the power to get wealth was given by God to establish His covenant on the earth. It's the challenge for Christian businesspeople to win them to Christ and have them working for the Kingdom of Light. Without resources, there is no sustainable ministry.

Church leaders, never forget, your businesspeople are more than your private ATM to fund all your church projects. They want to—and will—support you, but you are called by God to equip them for their call to create wealth and influence the world of business. The more the keepers of the business gate prosper, the more the Kingdom of God advances.

Second, the government gate. These are our God-ordained legislators. They pass the laws and regulations that control our society and culture. I've heard church leaders all my life say, stay out of politics. It's corrupt and dirty. Pray for them, yes. But don't get involved.

How did politics become so corrupt and evil? The Church walked away and was no longer a part. Sad to say, corrupt Church leaders and an out-of-control humanistic government have been in bed together for the past eighty years.

High-profile evangelical leaders refuse to take on the battle publicly while preaching a culturally compromising gospel. If you want to know where evil politicians are taking us, simply read the Humanist Manifesto I and II.

Third, the education gate. Our educators determine the values, philosophy, and worldview of every succeeding generation. According to the authors of *None Dare Call It Education* (John A. Stormer) and *Bending the Twig* (Augustin G. Rudd), our children's education is no longer primarily learning the arts and sciences, but rather social indoctrination and being politically correct.

The National Education Association, America's strongest and wealthiest union, is determined to obliterate every visage of God, Christianity, and the Bible from the classroom—from the nursery school to the university. The NEA is well-funded and has made it its life's purpose to indoctrinate our children with anti-God philosophy until they can no longer see any difference between right or wrong.

They believe there is no absolute truth, as all is relative. Truth is what you believe it to be, regardless of how much it brings harm and heartache.

Why Are We Not Possessing the Gates of Our Enemy?

> "For the kingdom of heaven is like a landowner who went out early in the morning to hire laborers for his vineyard. Now when he had agreed with the laborers for a denarius a day, he sent them into his vineyard. And he went out about the third hour and saw others standing idle in the marketplace, and said to them, 'You also go into the vineyard, and whatever is right I will give you.' So, they went.
>
> Again he went out about the sixth and the ninth hour, and did likewise. And about the eleventh hour he went out and found others standing idle, and said to them, 'Why have you been standing here idle all day?' They said to him, 'Because no hired us.' He said to them, 'You also go into the vineyard, and whatever is right you will receive.' (Matthew 20:1–7 NKJV)

The Church goes to the marketplace every day. Some still have secular jobs, and some have had the revelation they no longer have a job—they have a calling and a ministry. Church leader, it's up to you to help them understand the difference. You will never see the transformation of your city as long as you keep sending laypeople to secular jobs.

Since Constantine became Emperor of Rome, the Church began to buy into Cessationism, meaning that certain gifts and experiences critical to the early Church and the advancement of Christianity no longer exists. As a result, Church leaders started teaching poor marketplace theology while creating a class system using such terms such as clergy, laity, full-time, part-time, bi-vocational, and other nonbiblical designations.

Much of this has led to the Church having little significant influence where it's needed most, in the harvest field we call the marketplace.

Ephesians 4 has great implications for marketplace ministry. There are those God has called to train and equip His warriors. And there are those He has called to execute His strategies to reap the harvest and build an ever-increasing army to possess the gates of our enemy. Neither role is more or less significant and critical to the task. It should not be an either/or choice.

Ministry should not be about geography or location but calling and awareness, whether it's the church house, office, shop, or classroom. In Hebrews, the Apostle Paul said not to forsake assembling together. However, Jesus said to go into the highways and byways. In the Matthew 20 text, the laborers seemed more concerned about wages than activity.

Pastors, it's up to you to persuade your marketplace ministers that the harvest must always be the motivation for going out to the fields every day, not monetary gain. The Greek word for "idle" in 20:6 is *Argos*, meaning "free from labor, at leisure, lazy, and shunning the work that has been assigned."

As Church leaders, you can't train them for their job (platform for their ministry) to which God has called them. But you can surely equip them for Kingdom ministry while they are there.

Another reason for idleness in the marketplace is that the Church is confused about marketing the Gospel and evangelism. Marketing is creating a sense of urgency and increasing demand. Evangelism—sales—is closing the deal.

The Church has tried to create a sense of urgency in the church house but has been unable to close the transaction in the marketplace. With few exceptions, Church leaders do not adequately prepare its members for evangelism or possess a clear strategy for taking back influence in the marketplace of their city.

It's admirable to reach out and meet the social and spiritual needs of your city, but the purpose of your church in your city is transforming the culture—changing it from an anti-God and humanistic influence to one that glorifies God and establishes His covenant promises.

The pastor/teacher gifts alone cannot produce that transformation. Transformation does not take place until all five Ephesians 4 gifts work together under the leadership of the apostolic gift. I have little use for titles and offices.

Those too many times have been used to gain power and prestige and put Christians in bondage—but accomplished very little in transforming cities and discipling nations. A title and name plaque on your office door does not guarantee the gift is present. Only the gift produces significant and sustainable fruit.

Ephesians 4 teaches that in the Ascension Gifts resides the full expression of Christ. He is the sum total of apostle, prophet, evangelist, pastor, and teacher. Because Christ is Head of the Church and the Church is His body and in Him, "we live and move and have our being" (Acts 17:28 NIV).

It makes sense that every local assembly would want to reflect His wholeness. Reflect it first within their own fellowship and then with those the Holy Spirit schedules Divine appointments every day.

The Holy Spirit came not only to teach us more about Christ and empower us to serve His body, but also to show His love to the world. All through the Gospels, the early Church demonstrated the fullness of Christ through Spirit-empowered, gifted believers. For the first three hundred years, the growth and development of the "called-out ones" centered around fully embracing and exercising these five supernatural gifts as living witnesses.

> Only God determines your gift.

Today's church is not struggling for lack of titles and positions, but for saints who know their gifting and how to use it serving their spiritual family, communicating God's love, and finishing His mission. Education, personality, and passion may enhance your gift, but they do not determine it. Even surrounding needs do not determine your gift.

Only God determines your gift. And it's your gift that determines where you are most effective, meet the most needs, and have the greatest Kingdom influence.

God's calling on your life will always exploit the gift He gave you. Frustrated, weary, and restless Christians are usually trying to serve God outside their gifting, both in the Body and the marketplace.

No amount of effort and perseverance, or even a change of geography, will overcome those feelings. The joy, peace, and fulfillment so desired in our calling comes from doing what God has gifted us to do, not what others think we ought to do.

The level of effectiveness of any local assembly is determined by the apostolic gift, regardless of what title they give their leader. It's the apostolic gift, building and supporting the other four gifts as a team, that brings strength, maturity, and unity and produces a battle-ready army.

"Equipping the saints" without understanding their gifts breeds redundancy and disappointment at best, or worst—confusion and mission failure. When a local church is deficient or impotent in any given area, rest assured it's lacking in the gift God assigned to meet that need.

- Without the apostolic gift, you have an unfathered church—one lacking a compelling vision and strategic leadership.

- Without the prophetic gift, you have an uncorrected church—one that lacks discipline, is unruly, and is unable to handle correction.

- Without the teaching gift, you have an untaught church—one lacking a strong biblical foundation while partial truths and false doctrine abound.

- Without the pastoral gift, you have an unshepherded church—one lacking compassion, spiritual healing, and a sense of family.

- Without the evangelist gift, you have an unpopulated church—one lacking passion for the lost and a steady flow of new converts.

The evangelist cares about how many say "yes" to Jesus. The pastor cares about how many are receiving care for hurts and wounds. The teacher cares about how many are growing in the Word and faith. The prophet cares about how many are living holy. The apostle cares about it all and builds a team to ensure that it happens.

> Evangelism is where it all starts.

Evangelism is where it all starts. However, without all five gifts operating in harmony, you are simply populating an army that has sons without fathers, is living in rebellion, lacks biblical understanding, is broken and hurting, and cannot reproduce itself.

Jesus said, "I will build my church [using all five gifts] and the gates [places of influence] of hell will not prevail." (Matthew 16:18)

Early Marketplace Ministry Strategies

Jesus repeatedly uses the term "marketplace," but somehow the Church continually fails to comprehend how important it is to world evangelism and discipling the nations. Jesus refused to involve Himself in the ecclesiastical system and seemed to go out of His way to avoid it.

Early Church leaders, especially the Apostle Paul, were anything but idle in the marketplace. By the third century, institutional concerns took precedence over efforts to impact the marketplace in any significant way.

Church indoor meetings, led by religious managers, found a way to keep everyday Christians busy in the building, and their marketplace activities and influence became less and less. Note Jesus's words in Luke 7:31–34 (NLT):

> "To what can you compare the people of this generation?" Jesus asked. "How can I describe them?" They are like children playing a game in the public square ["marketplace" in KJV]. They complain to their friends, 'We played wedding songs, and you didn't dance, so we played funeral songs, and you didn't weep.
>
> For John the Baptist did not spend his time eating bread and drinking wine, and you say, 'He's possessed by a demon.' The Son of Man, on the other hand, feasts and drinks and you say, 'He's a glutton and a drunkard, and a friend of tax collectors and other sinners!'"

Jesus was describing the religious leaders of His day as children sitting around in the marketplace, complaining. They didn't have a clue who John or Jesus were and why they came. It seems we have a similar situation today.

The Church goes to great lengths to describe and define our anti-Christ culture but lacks any clear strategy on how to change it. The prophets keep predicting what God's going to do some day according to Scripture, but the apostolic gift is silent on how marketplace ministers, the warriors who go to the frontlines every day, can effect change.

Ezekiel went to great lengths in describing marketplace activities in Tyre, the center of economic activity in his day, and how God's people were falling down on the job. Today's Church seems to be more interested with advertising what's happening inside their walls while neglecting marketplace opportunities all around them.

> Invading the darkness and gathering the harvest should be a way of life, not an occasional event.

Marketing internal Church activities does little in creating marketplace activity. Our enemy is not the least bit concerned with the size of our meeting facilities, how many attend our meetings, and the size of our institutional budget.

What does threaten his kingdom of darkness is how many well-trained warriors the Church sends to invade and take back ground that rightfully belongs to our King, the King of Righteousness. Promoting church events should never replace our passion for marketplace influence and destroying the works of the devil.

Invading the darkness and gathering the harvest should be a way of life, not an occasional event. Marketing the Kingdom of Light searches out the unreached people or groups. Evangelism communicates the uncompromised message in a relevant way. Discipleship completes the transaction and creates a lifetime follower of Jesus Christ.

True evangelism shares the Gospel with those who have never heard. It's the revivalist who travels from church to church stirring up the saints. Gifted evangelists seldom travel.

Yet their schedule remains full. We call it marketplace evangelism.

Church leaders, your main calling is to energize your idle marketplace warriors. Most don't know what to do, how to do it, or even why they go to the marketplace outside of earning an income to support their family and the church they attend.

Most cannot see a direct correlation between what they hear on Sundays and what they face on Mondays. Traditional church models and leaders must change that, or marketplace ministers remain idle and the laborers for Kingdom advancement remain unemployed.

Your marketplace ministers have been called to one of three places of service: business, government, or education. It's your job to help them find God's purpose for being there and how to be effective. You must help them stop compartmentalizing their lives between secular versus sacred. Those compartments don't exist in God's world, and they should not in ours.

Your life as a church leader and their lives as a marketplace minister must be the integration of all the God-given opportunities woven into a seamless life lived to the glory of God, regardless of where you live out your priesthood. The Bible says our whole life was planned before we were born, and our steps are ordered of the Lord for His service.

If that is the case, how can we have both secular and sacred parts to our lives? I believe this kind of thinking has done more to hold back world evangelism and fulfilling the Church's purpose and mission more than any other single reason.

Richard C. Halverson (Chaplain, United States Senate, 1981–1995) made the following quote in his 1981 book, *Walk With God Between Sundays*:

> "The Church has succeeded in pulling Christians out of the world, out of society and out of civic affairs. So often the Church is a little island of piety surrounded by an ocean of need. Our preoccupation with the establishment has been so complete that we have been unable to see the ocean. Except of course, if there is someone out there that we want to recruit for our program. The congregation has become an exclusive little system of satellites orbiting our programs."

How many lights does a lighting store need? The biblical goal of informed church leaders managing the lighting store is producing spiritually and emotionally mature warriors who take their place as lights in a dark world. Ones that are ambassadors in a hostile environment. Messengers to an uninformed society. Hope-dealers to a hopeless society, and M.D.s—Mighty Delivers—to the sick, wounded, and devastated.

The question is not, "How involved are you using your lamps in the lighting store? And do you light up every time the store is open?" The question should be, "How well are the leaders of your church lighting store equipping you to use your lamp to light up the dark areas where you go every week in the marketplace?" If they aren't fulfilling their Ephesians 4 assignment, why do you continue to follow?

Church leaders must continue to produce people whose ordinary stations in life are transformed into opportunities to share the love of God and extend His Kingdom principles throughout the earth resulting in the discipling of all nations.

This cannot be accomplished in one or two meetings a week, even every night of the week or by a handful of professionals. Every believer has been called, gifted, and assigned to not just reach the lost and disciple them in the Word, but also to train in the art of spiritual warfare, executed from their platform of marketplace ministry.

> "A city set on a hill cannot be hidden; nor do people light a lamp and put it under a basket, but on the lampstand, and it gives light to all who are in the house." (Matthew 5:14–15 NASB)

Visibility is always the issue. How many lamps do you need in a lighting store? Not many, but every Christian is called to shine where it's darkest. Church leader, it's your God-given assignment to help them make that happen. Marketplace ministers, your marketplace calling is your lampstand. Make sure you are not a flashlight used only in emergencies. Don't be a strobe light: lots of glitter, but inconsistent at best.

Be a mature Christian searchlight, not looking for sin in peoples' lives, but showing them a path out of the darkness, disappointment, and despair—common to so many that God brings across your path every day. This only happens when the lamps leave the lighting store and leave their light on.

I have been developing leaders, building teams, and finding solutions in both the church world and the marketplace for many years. I've seen God draw men's souls to the message of the Cross and do signs and wonders in both. In this chapter, I have shared my heart and I pray that the message has reached yours.

The Bible says, the harvest is great and the laborers, those who understand why God called them to the marketplace, are few. However, it's time we affirm, develop, and deploy the 95% who will never fill a pulpit. They have a call and a platform in the marketplace, the first-century mission field, and the twenty-first century's greatest opportunity. I close with some practical ways you can make your church Ephesians 4:1–friendly:

- Map your city or area indicating where your E41 ministers live out their Ephesians 4:1 assignment.
- Schedule regular onsite visits with your E41 ministers for support and encouragement.
- Have "How I connect Sunday to Monday" testimonies often.
- Develop a solid biblical theology for work and marketplace ministers. Teach and preach on it regularly.
- Commission your E41 ministers after their E41 training in a special service.
- Conduct an annual "Marketplace Ministers" conference and Sunday where everyone comes dressed in their marketplace ministry uniforms.
- Put the tools of Ephesians 4:1 ministers on display as a way of honoring them and their calling.
- Discontinue "dismissing" your services and release them to ministry.
- Post signs over all exit doors, "Service Entrance."

These are just a few ways you can recognize and affirm those who answered the Ephesians 4:1 call, gone through the training, and go to the front lines every day. Ask God to give you even more creative ways to encourage, affirm, and support these great men and women. I salute you for all efforts to extend God's Kingdom in your city.

Questions for Reflection and Application

1. The author challenges us that if we want to see our cities transformed, we need to see the full complement of Ephesians 4 equipping gifts functioning. How intentional are you in nurturing all these gifts? If you had to identify the gifting and function that is the most conspicuously absent, which would it be?

2. If God wants righteous people manning the gates of business, government, and education, how can you be intentional in equipping the frontline warriors in this battle?

3. The author says, "Church leaders, your main calling is to energize your idle marketplace warriors. Most don't know what to do, how to do it, or even why they go to the marketplace outside of earning an income to support their family and the church they attend." Brainstorm three things you could start right away that would begin to change this.

Dr. David Robinson has developed his leadership and management skills since 1966 through a wide range of opportunities in both the church world and the marketplace. He and his wife, Marie, have been married since 1968 and have three children, eight grandchildren, and three great grandchildren. They have lived in the Chicago, Illinois, area since 1979.

Dr. Robinson has a Bachelor of Applied Theology from Logos Christian College, Master of Organizational

Leadership from Southern Seminary, and a Ph.D. in Organizational Leadership from Logos University. He also serves on the Board of Regents for Logos University and is an Adjunct Professor in the area of leadership. He is a Certified Trainer for *The Five Languages of Appreciation for the Workplace* by Gary Chapman and Paul White.

Since 2005, he has served as a full-time executive leadership coach for leaders in the church, business, government, and education. He travels in the United States and overseas 200+ days a year helping leaders improve their leadership skills and see their vision become a reality.

He has authored many top-selling books, including *Idle in the Marketplace at the Eleventh Hour, 50 Leadership Keys That Work, 100 Leadership Nuggets,* and *The Abominable Snowman.* He also wrote *Possessing the Gates of Your Enemy,* a definitive work on Marketplace Ministry. He publishes a monthly e-Leadership article currently read by 40,000+ people in over thirty nations. You can also follow him on Twitter and Facebook.

9

Equipping for the Other 4 C's:
How Pastors Can Equip Their Members Beyond Church Service for Community, City, Career, and Culture Influence

Joseph Umidi

One of the major transitions in my calling as a pastor, equipper, church planter, ministry professor, apostolic overseer, and leadership coach trainer was to move the goalposts. I thought my primary role was to equip the saints for the work of the ministry in the Church. What a delight and discovery to add the other 4 C's in this chapter title to my definition of success.

Reading the Research

A key milestone of my own transition was the research that showed the major disconnect between what Bible schools and seminary teachers were working hard to form in their students and what the members in the churches were expecting from their pastors.

The blockbuster ATS Murdock Report in 1994[6] pointed out that the top five things expected from seminary profs and the top five things expected from church parishioners did not even match!

---

[6] This study was challenging to the ATS accreditors and is now hard to find, though there have been several interpretations of the results, including those in power who tried to minimize those findings. My summary is subjective to what I perceived as the bottom-line findings. Several DMin. dissertations came out of this.

Seminary Profs	Church Members
Exegeting the Bible	Family survive, thrive in the culture
Casting vision for the Church	Clarifying my calling
Managing church systems	Accelerating my vocational impact
Training volunteer for church growth	Equipping for transforming 4 C's
Attending discipleship classes	Measuring my maturity progress

A survey of over 10,000 members of a church network surprised the pastors when their members responded as to a key focus they needed from their church staff. "We need to know how we are doing at being disciples and making disciples from year to year. We keep showing up to all the church meetings but no one in leadership is helping us see any progress in our tailor-made individual development."[7]

A recent work by *Church for Monday* author Dr. Svetlana Papazov[8] noted how to change the scorecard for pastoral success from a church-centric to a Kingdom-centric focus. That would include the following:

Bodies: Count the people reached during the week versus on Sunday morning.

Bucks: Count the economic development the church causes versus only the budget.

Buildings: Count the ways that church facilities touch people during the week versus on weekends.

---

[7] This is from the Willow Creek Association well before the scandal of the founder stepping down from leadership.

[8] See page 124 from *Church for Monday: Equipping Believers for Mission at Work*.

Kent Humphrey's two-volume series called *Shepherding Horses* makes helpful distinctions between members/influencers or volunteers/leaders. There is a distinction that pastors must make between the traditional mindset of discipling sheep from horses. That includes the following equipping advice[9]:

1. Call them into a personal relationship with you.
2. Create an atmosphere of understanding with them.
3. Affirm them in their workplace calling.
4. Equip them as ministers in the workplace.
5. Commission them as a world ambassador for Christ.
6. Release them for service in their own sphere of influence.

All the above can help us understand why we are hearing more of these statements from disillusioned church members than ever:

"How come my pastor does not connect with me in my world?"

"It seems that my pastor has not embraced the "work of the ministry" outside of the "ministry of the church."

"We have not felt validated or honored in our role as 'saints' outside the 'gathering of the saints'."

"We rarely see an attempt to integrate the 'vision of the house' with the 'calling of the members'."

---

[9] *Shepherding Horses*, Volume I, pages 414–511.

Rereading the Scripture

The book of Ephesians has been called the constitution of the church. For years, I designed and taught the flagship course at Regent University School of Divinity called Church and Ministry. The foundational verse for that course is Ephesians 4:11–13 (NKJV):

> And He Himself gave some to be apostles, some prophets, some evangelists, and some pastors and teachers, ¹² for the equipping of the saints for the work of ministry, for the edifying of the body of Christ, ¹³ till we all come to the unity of the faith and of the knowledge of the Son of God, to a perfect man, to the measure of the stature of the fullness of Christ;

Notice some elements of this passage that speak to the 4 C's of our title.

First, all five "functions" are gifts to the church (Ephesians 5:8) and are critical to every local church in the call to equip. Notice, I did not say all five "offices," nor all five "titles."

The five-fold functions are what is needed to be sure that we are recruiting, raising up, and releasing disciples who are equipped and imparted to by those who have the capacity in their function.

These can be called Five-Fold Fathers/Mothers in the faith who must be recruited by their pastors to be an integral part of the equipping mandate of the church.

The challenge has been that we have left the equipping to only the pastor and teacher. That results in most of the equipping being focused on the ministry of the church and to the church.

The primary equipping for the ministry outside of the church needs to be accomplished by those who express their primary ministry outside of the church walls.

That is the "APE" missing factor in most churches; the apostolic, prophetic, and evangelistic. In many ways, those who function in the APE stream are the "horses" and not the "sheep." When the goal of the equipping is to make better sheep rather than better horses, we have better church members but not better influencers outside of the church walls.

Authors Hirsch and Catchim[10] express Ephesians 4 in sociological terms that help us get outside our church bubble focus to embrace the APE foundation. Here is how they put it:

> "Apostles in the generic sense are those sent out to pioneer something new—for example, teachers who are called in to turn failing schools around, along with people who start movements of sorts, architect systems, or start entrepreneurial business ventures.
>
> Prophets tend to be visionaries, but in a very different sense; they often have a keen interest in issues of justice, environmental responsibility, or the creative arts.
>
> Evangelists are particularly gifted at enthusing others about what they stand for, selling the significance of their work, company, or product outside the group itself. These are easy to spot—the United States is full of them."

---

[10] See *The Permanent Revolution: Apostolic Imagination and Practice for the 21st Century Church*, pg. 9.

Because the foundation of the church is built on the apostles and prophets (Ephesians 2:20), we may need to restore their role on building our people and our church in the 4 C's opportunity.

Reframing Operating in Our Unique Anointing Identity

Any pastor will automatically be able to answer this core question: What did the anointing of the Spirit cause Jesus to be and do?

> "The Spirit of the LORD is upon Me,
> Because He has anointed Me
> To preach the gospel to the poor;
> He has sent Me to heal the brokenhearted,
> To proclaim liberty to the captives
> And recovery of sight to the blind,
> To set at liberty those who are oppressed;
> To proclaim the acceptable year of the LORD."
> (Luke 4:18–19 NKJV)

"When do I get to do this stuff?" the late John Wimber once asked of his pastor. The simple answer is whenever anyone member of the Body of Christ is anointed to do so. What a privilege for everyone to do this anyplace, anytime, to anyone!

The tougher answer comes when we ask this question: "When the Spirit of the Lord is upon me in the 4 C's of my day-to-day life, what does the anointing cause me to be and do?"

Reframing the anointing outside of preaching, healing, and liberating allows our church members to move in the anointing in the boardroom, school playground, office suite, watercooler, and any other 4 C context opportunity. They get to do this stuff through the unique identity that matches the unique culture in which they labor.

But wait, there is more. Because we are "fearfully and wonderfully made marvelous in God's sight" (paraphrase of Psalm 139), we have a unique, one-of-a-kind creation design that the new creation work of the Holy Spirit most regularly activates us to be and do what cannot be accomplished on our own strength.

> Our own identity under the anointing is our tailor-made power!

In other words, we can be naturally supernatural, without quoting chapter and verse, to our coworkers, vendors, and clients that does not require us to wear Saul's armor for battle. Our own identity under the anointing is our tailor-made power!

Jack worked his way up to become a top-gun pilot. Today, he will tell you that his unique anointing experienced daily is as a fourth-grade teacher at his local school.

Shaping the next generation in teachable moments is when he abundantly senses the pleasure of God in his vocation. "This is what I was designed to do, and I am glad I am able to express it," is his message to us.

Jack needed a pastor who honored and called forth that unique anointing in him, rather than a one-size-fits-all approach to his parishioners. Here is how he equipped Jack through these powerful questions:[11]

---

[11] Question taken from the Dreamfire Experience, found at www.lifeformingcoach.com.

"When are you most naturally engaged and animated in your daily life?"

"What ignites your creativity?"

"What would those closest to you say you are most passionately anointed about?"

"What makes you come most fully alive spiritually, emotionally, and physically?"

"What spiritual stirrings keep you up at night?"

Releasing Transformational Culture Agents

As a pastor, I have modeled and multiplied a sending commissioning opportunity whenever we gather corporately. That is defined as a) being willing to be an agent for the Kingdom whenever you are starting a new year, a new beginning, or traveling to a new territory; b) receiving prayer for that; and c) reporting back to those who prayed for you and those providing support, encouragement, and accountability in that sending.

The powerful statement of Isaiah when he said, "Here am I. Send me!" (Isaiah 6:8 NIV) should not be just between you and Jesus, but it should also be the responsibility and privilege of your local church leadership as in Acts 13:2–4a (NKJV):

> As they ministered to the Lord and fasted, the Holy Spirit said, "Now separate to Me Barnabas and Saul for the work to which I have called them." ³Then, having fasted and prayed, and laid hands on them, **they sent** them away. ⁴So, being **sent out by the Holy Spirit...**

This three-way partnership of the church leadership, the church member, and the Holy Spirit brings a validation and a spiritual authority to the 4 C's that empowers church members.

It brings every profession to a higher place of honor rather than that usually given to only church planters and missionaries.

It helps break the boredom and monotony of our careers by being more fully aware and alive to the Kingdom opportunities that God has already prepared for each of us in our daily lives. In an era where 73% of workers and even CEOs do not look forward to going to work, this is a key for our members to make a living doing what they love, or learn to return to their first love of their work.

There is a shift in spiritual perspective when we are sent and a laser focus on creating or seizing the "purpose moments" that are there by God's design ahead of time. When our church members are honored for their unique calling, they are more able to create honor in the cultures they are called to influence.

I worked for seven years in a small Canadian city with an honor deficit in the stories that gave meaning to their culture. From the very foundation of their town, there was a major injustice that created a culture of dishonor and was still affecting two people groups hundreds of years later.

Two cultures and language groups occupied this city in almost a 50/50 ratio, but the stories of noncooperation, distrust, prejudice, and stereotypes were deeply ingrained in the psyche of the people. It was evident to an outsider that they had come to accept living in this murky fish tank as if it were normal and it was all they could ever expect.

After being captivated by the stories in Alex Haley's classic *Roots*, I teamed up with some leaders to determine how we could shift the culture to one of more honor. We invited all the elderly members of the community, with their own roots for generations, to find some of the oldest pictures and artifacts from their family and come to a community hall we rented for a Saturday Roots Day.

> As a pastor, I have modeled and multiplied a sending commissioning opportunity whenever we gather corporately.

With almost two hundred card tables set up with fine linen, each of them brought the items that told the stories of the past as we filled the hall with the lineage of the community's pioneers. In addition, we marketed to the entire community to come and visit them on this day and hear the stories of the people who had dreamed and sacrificed to make this community viable.

Something transformational and sustainable happened that day. The elderly received the gift of honor by us and, more importantly, by the community residents who had no idea of the past and how it always affects the present. Conversations went to a meaningful level, talking of dreams realized and yet to be fulfilled.

In this multigenerational and multicultural moment in time, something shifted in the way people viewed each other—moving toward a visible respect and reverence. From that moment on, we gained a momentum that enabled us to build a model of community transformation that included the businesses and local government for years to come.[12]

Reworking Our Monthly Schedules to Fulfill the 4 C's

So, what would be an ideal month in the life of a pastor who is equipping their members for Community, City, Career, and Culture Influence? It all begins with these time-tested methods of "watch and pray," "listen to what really matters," and discerning the spirits that our members face in their environments.

There is a guaranteed way to prioritize this in the lives of pastors; be incarnational according to what Jesus modeled in Philippians 2:5–8. Leave the perspective of the church organizational world behind daily to enter the world of our members. Be "with them" in a "with reach" mindset to discover what they need to flourish.

Here is a model that can touch the seven key spheres of influence our members need to be equipped to impact:

> **Month 1:** Show up at local high schools to enter the world of the principal, teachers, workers, and students. Quietly prayer walk with them to gain spiritual insight that only comes onsite.
>
> Prepare for a powerful conversation with them to collaboratively discover how to exegete that culture. Meet with their coworkers as you ask the Holy Spirit to find the men and women of peace who will welcome you.

---

[12] See pages 5–6 from this author's *Transformational Intelligence: Creating Cultures of Honor at Home and Work.*

Month 2: Seek the welfare of your city by finding ways to enter the world of the city municipal center. Meet with the mayor and other board members.

Ask them what the toughest problems are that they face. Commit to helping them find solutions and offer to find others to serve.

Ask if you can mobilize prayer for them with only their commitment to inform you when that which is prayed for is happening. Have a theology that God is eager to answer the felt needs of these workers in order to reveal His character and grace to them.

Month 3: Ask for a tour of your local/regional media station and be ready to compliment them beforehand on something they do right (no matter how much they do wrong, in your opinion). Ask them lots of questions, including:

> What led you into this work?
> What is the most fulfilling part of your day?
> What would you want our young people to know about your work before pursuing this as a career?
> Who do look up to in this industry, and what would you want to be your legacy?

Ask them if you could pray for them until your next meeting. Also, ask then what would be on their list of concerns.

Month 4: Ask the members of your church who are artistic to point you to those in the community/city who are influencers. Ask if you can interview them and if they can meet with your members on what questions to develop.

See if you can let them know how you understand their role in culture and that you appreciate their attempt to steward that seriously.

Develop a relationship with a few in which you can sincerely ask them about the creative process and how they feel inspired. Seek to develop a theology of beauty that can build bridges for your church artists to have credibility in their eyes. See yourself as an artistic bridge builder.

Month 5: Survey how many in your church are small businessmen and women and how many work in the corporate arena. Meet with them in groups to see how you can help them with a biblical view of wealth, generosity, and stewardship. Resource them with those who have time-tested powerful teachings on these topics.[13]

Honor them for the faith necessary to do business God's way. Ask them how they can be covered in prayer for the major battles they face in this economy. Ask them how the church can help them with their families and the time they

---

[13] See the author's site www.imagination.partners for resources on Family Generational Wisdom and free resources on online business initiatives.

need to give them, when there is so much to do in their businesses.

Month 6: Meet for Sunday meals with at least one or more families (group) per week to explore the dynamics they face in marriage and parenting. Offer to help them find resources to support them and stories of those who have weathered the storms of contemporary culture pressures.

Make sure than none of their children leave home without the help and resources to know who they are and why they are here, including their critical need for financial intelligence.[14]

Month 7: Meet with your key leaders to study and implement a transformational process of maturing disciples and multiplying leaders that emphasizes these first six monthly components.

Agree in faith and make declarations that healthy members in the above six areas will create a healthy and growing church without revolving doors. Bring in other pastors and leaders who focus in the 4 C's and let them tell their stories to your leadership.

---

[14] See the author's site www.imagination.partners for resources on Funancial Freedom training for middle school and high school-age family members before they leave home.

Questions for Reflection and Application

1. Dr. Umidi gives evidence of the disconnect between pastors and church members. What impact is this disconnect having on the church and the world, and how can we reconnect?

2. The author talks about the importance of sending transformational cultural agents. In what ways are you sending people to engage the 4C's?

3. The author provides a sample month-by-month plan to engage the 4C's. What in your church, tradition, culture, or experience is holding you back from implementing something like this?

Dr. Joseph Umidi serves as Executive Vice President at Regent University, having also served as Interim Dean and Professor during his thirty-five years of service. He has researched and discovered keys to accelerate student retention and has trained all the university staff in developing a culture of honor.

During this tenure, he has served in senior leadership roles of several churches. He is Founder and President of Lifeforming Leadership Coaching, Inc., a coach training organization in twenty-nine countries and fourteen languages. He has authored numerous articles and books dealing with organizational and personal transformation and is working in Financial Wellness for families and churches. He is married to Marie, Founder & President of TMCJ, Inc., and they are the delighted grandparents of three grandchildren.

www.lifeformingcoach.com
www.imagination.partners

10
The Faith@Work Movement in America
Os Hillman

The faith at work movement has its early beginnings in 1930. That year, CBMC (Connecting Businessmen to Christ), a non-charismatic marketplace ministry, was birthed and continues today with a focus on evangelism to men in the marketplace. In 1952, the Full Gospel Businessmen's Fellowship International was birthed through Demos Shakarian. These two organizations represent the focus of workplace ministry over the last fifty years. That focus has largely been on executives, men, and evangelism.

These ministries were birthed outside the local church and have often been seen by church leaders as competition to the local church. Dozens of ministries birthed in the mid-1990s such as the Halftime Institute, Pinnacle Forum, and Marketplace Leaders, to name a few of the dozens. These started because the local church failed to understand or embrace the average person's passion to reflect their faith in the workplace.

In the last twenty years, there has been a new paradigm in workplace ministry unfolding. Twenty years ago, we could identify only twenty-five formalized workplace ministries. Today, we have identified 1,200 organizations that seek to integrate faith and work around the world. These include nonprofit workplace ministries, educational institutions, business organizations, and churches that intentionally focus on faith and work.

This incredible rate of growth is why many are saying that there is a genuine move of God taking place in this arena that has the potential for changing the spiritual landscape in the local church, cities, and nations. If we ever needed revival in America, it is now.

One of the key differences in the modern-day movement is that the focus is no longer evangelism to male executives. The modern-day movement is focused on a more holistic approach to applying faith in the realm where so many people spend so much of their time—their work life. These include students, stay-at-home spouses and parents, those in the military, executives, nurses, doctors, lawyers, and people in entertainment and government.

> Have you ever considered that Jesus modeled workplace ministry?

Ministries are no longer just birthing outside the local church as parachurch ministries. Now, local churches are also recognizing the need to equip their people and release them into their workplaces as extended missions of their churches.

There is a trumpet call to return to the early church model of biblical ministry that resides with every believer. This call is to the 9-to-5 window, where there are more unreached people residing than in the 10/40 window. It is a movement that is designed to change the 80/20 rule in the local church—from 20% of people doing ministry to 80%.

And most of all, it is a movement that is designed to ignite transformation in lives, churches, cities, and nations. Many believe it may be how the Lord will bring genuine revival into our nations because those in the workplace often reside in the place of authority in our cities—and have the ability to make significant changes in the way things are done.

If there was ever a time we needed a *tipping point*, it is now. The faith at work movement has the potential to tip the scale from a nation that is falling away from its spiritual roots to a nation that returns to its spiritual destiny. Unless there is a tipping point toward God, America will fall to Marxism and socialism and become a completely secular nation.

> **Jesus was a workplace minister who combined both a priestly call with a workplace call.**

Have you ever considered that Jesus modeled workplace ministry? It is easy to forget that Jesus spent more than 50% of His adult life in a carpentry shop. He was more known for being a carpenter than He was for being the Son of God. Perhaps that is why so many people had difficulty reconciling Jesus the carpenter with Jesus the Son of God who did miracles in the workplace.

Consider the following amazing facts:

- The New Testament records that Jesus appeared publicly 132 times—122 were in the marketplace.
- Jesus told fifty-two parables—forty-five had a workplace context.
- Acts recorded forty divine interventions—thirty-nine were in the marketplace.
- Jesus spent His adult life as a carpenter until the age of thirty when He began a public preaching ministry in the workplace.
- Jesus called twelve workplace individuals—not clergy—to build His Church.

- Work is *worship*. The Hebrew word *Avodah* is the root word for both *work* and *worship*.
- Work in its different forms is mentioned more than eight hundred times in the Bible—more than all the words used to express *worship, music, praise*, and *singing* combined.

> "His doing nothing wonderful (his first 30 years) is in itself a kind of wonder." —Saint Bonaventure

Yes, Jesus was a workplace minister who combined both a priestly call with a workplace call. In the mind of Jesus, there was no sacred/secular divide. He did not consider His work life to be less important than His spiritual life. Both were entwined in everyday life. The Hebrews understood this. There was not a separation of *faith life* from *work life*.

Oswald Chambers, well-known author of *My Utmost for His Highest*, said, "The spiritual manifests itself in a life which knows no division into sacred and secular."

If you were to conduct a survey on an average city street and ask if religion belonged in the workplace, chances are high that most answers would be no—and that would be correct. *Religion* doesn't, but *Jesus* does.

Most people today, even many Christians, see no relevance between God and work in today's fast-paced society. Why is this? It goes back to the early years before the Protestant Reformation. It is understandable why we are where we are today. Throughout the centuries, we have been trained to believe that the two worlds of spiritual and secular are to be separated.

> May the favor of the LORD our God rest on us; establish the work of our hands for us—yes, establish the work of our hands. (Psalm 90:17 NIV)

Throughout the church, a view of those in "full-time" Christian work versus those who work "secular" jobs has created a definite class distinction. There seems to be little evidence of this distinction in the Bible. Yet, we often hear testimonies from those who left "regular" jobs to go into the mission field, or some other "full-time" Christian work.

It's time we equip men and women to see their work as a holy calling from God to be cultural influencers.

Pastor, could the following letter have been written by a marketplace servant (minister) from your congregation?

> Dear Pastor,
>
> For some time now I have felt the need to write you this letter. Let me first say I want to thank you for what you do in helping me learn more about how I can grow in my relationship with Jesus. Your contribution to my spiritual life is so important and is greatly appreciated.
>
> But, there are times I think that you and I may have a wrong view of each other. For instance, as a person in the workplace, I sometimes feel I may be valued for the financial contributions I can make, or the ministry position I can fill "at church." Pastor, this makes me feel disconnected and devalued. I know God has created me for a unique purpose, and like you, He has called me for a special ministry.

I know God has given me spiritual gifts and I believe that we should all contribute to the local church function, as well as to the broader Kingdom. Sometimes I feel that the church spends more time equipping me to do the church's ministry instead of my ministry. I love our church and I really have a heart to serve. Can you help me reconcile these feelings? I want to understand and fulfill my purpose—my life ministry.

God has begun to show me something very important. My work is my ministry. I feel that God has called me to be a minister at the workplace, in the same way He has called you to be a pastor. I really see my ministry at work as an extension of your ministry and our church. We don't often discuss ministry in this fashion, and sometimes I sense that my ministry at the workplace does not seem to fit the mission and philosophy of "ministry" in our church.

You see, I believe my ministry is to my coworkers who have never been inside a church building. They don't really relate to "church," so through work I may be the only "Jesus" they ever see. Pastor, I wish you could see the people here at work—they are so open to talking about spiritual things.

As I read the Bible, it seems like Jesus spent most of His time reaching people in the marketplace. You have taught me to follow His example, and I am finally beginning to understand what you have taught from Ephesians 4:11–12: "And He Himself gave some to be apostles, some prophets, some evangelists, and some pastors and teachers, for the equipping of the saints for the work of ministry."

> It seems like Jesus spent most of His time reaching people in the marketplace.

I agree with you, that as my pastor, God has assigned you the responsibility to equip me for "the work of ministry." God has revealed to me that my greatest ministry is at work. I need your help and training so that I can fulfill my "election" and calling. I know I need more biblical teaching about how to respond to this assignment to a vast, relatively untapped mission field.

Wouldn't it be great if I and other members of our church saw ourselves as "on a mission" at work? Christians taking a position of spiritual authority in the workplace! Just think of the impact the members of our church could make. This would be true multiplication!

Pastor, I know you have a desire to see our congregation reach more people for Christ. If we were committed to reaching the largest mission field in the world—our workplaces—just think what could be done.

Wow! It's exciting to imagine what God could do through an army of excited, motivated Christians accountable to the local church as workplace ministers. We might really begin to fulfill the Great Commission in a revolutionary way. Please Pastor, train us and send us out! Please consider commissioning those of us that are ready as fellow ministers in the workplace.

I love you and appreciate all that you do. I hope that together we can reach the people in my workplace.

Very truly yours,

Church Member

Questions for Reflection and Application

1. The author gives evidence of the incredible growth of workplace ministries—from 25 to over 1,200 in the last 20 years. What is God doing with this movement? Do you think the average church is aware of this?

2. How would you answer the Dear Pastor letter?

Os Hillman is president of Marketplace Leaders and is the author of *TGIF: Today God Is First,* and 23 other books on faith, work, and calling (www.TodayGodIsFirst.com).

Os Hillman owned and operated an ad agency from 1984 to 2001. During this time, he served clients such as American Express, Steinway Pianos, US Kids Golf, Peachtree Software, ADP Payroll Services, Parisian Department stores (now Belk), Thomas Nelson Publishers, and many nonprofit organizations. His company won many prestigious awards from the Direct Marketing Industry including the Echo Award, Direct Marketing's highest achievement for excellence in direct marketing for specific ad campaigns.

Os has been featured on CNBC, *The Los Angeles Times*, *The New York Times*, and many Christian media outlets. He has been a regular contributor to Crosswalk.com, *Charisma Leader* magazine, *Christian Post* and iDisciple. He has spoken at Harvard University and was a visiting professor at Regent University for a season.

Today, Os Hillman is president of Marketplace Leaders and Aslan Group Publishing, and is involved in several entrepreneur ventures related to publishing and internet marketing. He is the author of 24 books, and is a speaker, consultant, and recognized authority in the role that faith and ethics play in the marketplace. He authors a daily email newsletter entitled *TGIF: Today God Is First* that is read daily in 104 countries.

Os attended the University of South Carolina on a golf scholarship and was a golf professional for three years before going into business in 1980. Os attended Calvary Chapel Bible School. Os is married to Pamela and has one married daughter, Charis Brown. Pamela is founder and president of Life Changers Legacy, a ministry to men and women in prison. He and his wife live in Cumming, Georgia, a suburb of Atlanta, with their five dogs.

11

Apostolic Economics: Building the Ecosystems of Our Cities
James Kramer

Though our life experiences may not always reflect it, there is no lack in the Kingdom. Some very astute Christian leaders have estimated that it would cost several trillion dollars to see every nation discipled and the Great Commission fulfilled in our lifetime. If this is true, then we will not be able to fulfill the Great Commission through a donation model alone.

Instead, the Lord is breathing upon a fresh, multifaceted strategy to fund His purposes, and He is maturing and positioning His sons and daughters to execute this strategy. As He does this, we must have a correct understanding of how God views resources and provision and what His intentions are for them.

Plundering the Enemy

One part within the story of Gideon especially stands out. Judges 6:2–5 says the Midianites had so oppressed the people of Israel that they were hiding in caves. Every time they planted crops, their oppressors would steal them. The Midianites did not spare a living thing for the Israelites, but left them completely impoverished. God heard the Israelites' cries for help, and He raised up Gideon to deliver them.

Likewise, for too long the enemy has stolen the resources of the Kingdom. But the Lord does not tolerate that for very long. In Amos 9:14, He says, "I will restore the fortunes of my people Israel, and they shall rebuild the ruined cities and inhabit them;

they shall plant vineyards and drink their wine, and they shall make gardens and eat their fruit" (ESV).

Exodus 12:36 describes what happened as the people of Israel left Egypt: "The LORD had made the Egyptians favorably disposed toward the people, and they gave them what they asked for; so they plundered the Egyptians" (NIV).

This is a prophetic statement for the people of God right now. For too long, the enemy has stolen from us, but he does not get the last word. As we move in alignment with the Father and unity with one another, we get to plunder the enemy.

The Great Wealth Transfer

Proverbs 13:22 says, "...the wealth of the sinner is stored up for the righteous" (NASB). A transfer of wealth is coming into the Kingdom for the purpose of financing the final evangelization of the earth.

Dr. C. Peter Wagner, in his book *The Great Transfer of Wealth*, describes this coming financial transfer and what has hindered its release. In his opinion, seven issues must be addressed within the Body of Christ:

1. We have not had the right biblical government within the church.

2. We have not fully understood God's purpose for wealth.

3. We have not had the right attitude about wealth; a poverty mindset has persisted.

4. We have not had the full view of the church; we have overemphasized the Oikos (family) while neglecting the Ekklesia (government).

5. We have not recognized the apostles of the workplace.
6. We have not had an efficient infrastructure in place for management of funds.
7. We have not had an adequate administrative structure to facilitate distribution of funds.[15]

Thankfully, over the past few decades, the Holy Spirit has been shifting paradigms and mindsets to bring the Body of Christ into alignment regarding the first four issues noted above.

Toward point number five, groups like Marketplace Leaders, 10x Catalyst Groups, CBMC, Pinnacle Forum, CEO Forum, C12, Convene, FCCI, KBA, and Heaven in Business have made tremendous strides, raising up apostolic leaders throughout the marketplace and equipping them as change agents.

Kingdom-focused organizations like TrustBridge, National Christian Foundation, The Signatry, SweetBridge, Kingdom Investors, Global Thrive Index, Legatum, and Commissioned are right now being positioned to address the final two points—creating infrastructures and administrative processes to manage and facilitate Kingdom finances.

A New Kingdom Economy

Recently, a new breed of apostolic entrepreneurs has come on the scene. These are not merely Kingdom-based businesses that give their profits to local churches and ministries. That would simply be a continuation of the current existing

---

[15] C. Peter Wagner, *The Great Transfer of Wealth* (New Kensington, PA: Whitaker House, 2014), Kindle location 763 of 2602.

donation model. Instead, they are pioneering a new apostolic move in Kingdom finances.

The Holy Spirit is raising up entrepreneurs with new business models, witty inventions, technological breakthroughs, and highly profitable, sustainable revenue streams. These new Kingdom businesses exist to solve some of the world's greatest problems. At their missional core, they directly help fulfill the Great Commission while addressing human flourishing issues through for-profit models.

These new models allow for faster scaling and expansive impact in every sphere of culture. It is an apostolic move of God that leverages the strength of the marketplace to advance the Kingdom, and it's happening right now. The Lord is releasing Kingdom-advancing, sustainable revenue models to address nearly every issue that our cities and nations are facing today.

In addition, numerous people and groups have received specific assignments to build core components for a decentralized Kingdom financial system based on godly principles of abundance. This Kingdom system will be untethered from the world's financial system, which is under the control of the spirit of Mammon and is marked by fear, poverty, greed, and corruption. The attributes of the Kingdom system will be righteousness, peace, and joy (see Romans 14:17 NIV).

Apostolic Strategic Philanthropy

The Holy Spirit is raising up apostolic leaders and entrusting them with great wealth. These leaders are investing their finances in for-profit ventures as well as not-for-profit giving. The Lord has been shifting mindsets about generosity into a new apostolic strategic philanthropy.

Kenny Klepacki runs a fourth-generation family office and is one of these strategic apostolic philanthropists. Family offices like Kenny's and various Christian donor-advised funds have identified billions of dollars, currently in the hands of Christians, that are stalled on the sidelines. Reasons for this include:

1. Lack of transparency and visibility into the impact of their giving
2. Inability to find quality organizations that meet their giving criteria
3. Previous bad experiences with wasteful and inefficient organizations

Kenny states:

> Right now, Kingdom-minded people are looking for efforts that are measurable, attainable, practical and sustainable. If I'm going to give money to something, I want to know that I can measure its success. I want to see goals being achieved. If an organization constantly needs money and cannot sustain themselves, then I won't give to them. People keep their finances on the sidelines because the organizations they've given to in the past have broken their trust too many times.
>
> We need to be able to sift through the information and find truth. What are the data and numbers telling me? How can I make good decisions with my finances? We want to be able to see which metrics really drive impact. We are called to steward our wealth for the Kingdom and we are accountable to God for where we

invest it. The organizations that leverage our finances properly and effectively will receive more.[16]

The Lord is raising up strategic apostolic philanthropists who will effectively leverage the resources He has given them to accomplish His purposes. These philanthropists are looking for greater visibility and transparency into the impact of their giving. Organizations that demonstrate effective impact will be trusted with more.

This is reflective of Jesus's parable about stewardship in Luke 19. In it, we see unique principles regarding apostolic economics. In the story, a man of noble birth called ten of his servants and gave them each one mina, telling them to put his money to work until he came back. The story continues:

> He was made King, however, and returned home. Then he sent for the servants to whom he had given the money, in order to find out what they had gained with it. The first one came and said, "Sir, your mina has earned ten more." "Well done, my good servant!" his master replied. "Because you have been trustworthy in a very small matter, take charge of ten cities." The second came and said, "Sir, your mina has earned five more." His master answered, "You take charge of five cities." (Luke 19:15–19 NIV)

The servants in this story were wise enough to get their minas to work for them and earn them more. Kris Vallotton, Senior Associate Leader of Bethel Church, compares this story to the Parable of the Talents in Matthew 25.

---

[16] Kenny Klepacki, personal communication, May 2020.

In that parable, the master entrusted his wealth to his servants and returned home to find what they had done with it. To the faithful servants, he said, "You have been faithful with a few things; I will put you in charge of many things." (Matthew 25:21 NIV)

In Luke 19, however, Vallotton points out that because the servants were wise enough to figure out how to get their minas to earn them more minas, they were not just entrusted with things; they were also given cities.

> The Lord is looking for people who know His heart and will use these resources to enact His will. not theirs.

Servants in both stories received rewards, but some got stuff while others got cities. The difference was that in Matthew 25, they worked for money; in Luke 19, their money worked for them.[17]

The ones who were wise enough to get their money to work for them were entrusted with cities because they created wealth. Wealth is an ecosystem and cities require ecosystems in order to thrive. Therefore, those who are wise enough to create wealth and build ecosystems are wise enough to lead cities.

---

[17] Kris Vallotton, "The Parable of the Talents & Minas," Bethel.TV, January 18, 2019.

Wealth Is God's Idea

In the midst of current trending arguments villainizing capitalism as a system that creates an unfair distribution of wealth and power, it's important to remember that the idea of wealth creation originated with God. Deuteronomy 8:18 (NIV) says, "Remember the LORD your God, for it is He who gives you the ability to produce wealth, and so confirms His covenant..."

> These new Kingdom businesses exist to solve some of the world's greatest problems.

Every earthly economic model is based around principles of lack. Heaven's economy, however, is based on principles of abundance, and the Lord enables us to create wealth in order to advance the Kingdom so that all may flourish. This is both a great privilege and a great responsibility.

The Lord is looking for people who know His heart and will use these resources to enact His will, not theirs. These people are being called to deeper places of intimacy with Him, and He is rooting out the corruption and greed in their hearts so He can entrust them with more.

Underneath the current divisive rhetoric and global social chaos exists a deep longing for people to experience life, freedom, and opportunity. Finances are only one part of this, but they are an important part.

As Christians, we have an opportunity to repent of our agreement with the spirit of Mammon—with its greed and corruption—and begin leading in a new way that releases the abundance of Heaven. As we do this, we will see lives changed, cities transformed, nations healed and discipled, and the purposes of Heaven fulfilled.

Questions for Reflection and Application

1. What is the Church's role in casting vision and nurturing apostolic entrepreneurship?

2. The author describes billions of dollars that are "sidelined" because those with these funds struggle to find organizations that meet their giving criteria. As a leader, what can you do to work toward better stewarding wealth?

James Kramer is CEO and co-founder of Commissioned, Pneuma33 Creative, and World Changer Foundation. James believes that Christians should be on the leading edge of technology, innovation, and design. He believes Heaven holds the answer to every problem our world faces, and that Christians fueled by the power of the Holy Spirit can transform every sphere of culture. Over the last decade, James has helped position hundreds of businesses into greater levels of growth and impact in their industries.

With clients ranging from serial entrepreneurs to multibillion-dollar companies, James has a proven track record in recognizing market opportunities and effective brand strategies. He and his beautiful bride, Anna, live in Kansas City and lead multiple Kingdom enterprises together.

12

The Birth of iWork4Him
Jim Brangenberg

Before Jesus began His public ministry at around thirty years old, He was a career carpenter. God could have sent Him to any family in the world, but He chose to place Jesus in the family of a small business owner. Why? Because business was originally God's idea.

For much of my life, I was a small business owner. However, all I wanted to do was quit my job and work in the four walls of the church. Why? Because I felt called to ministry, and that is all I had ever been told ministry was—working in the church or the foreign mission field. No one ever said that God could use me as an insurance agent, IT guy, or used car dealer.

"Business is business, and church is church. They have nothing to do with each other. So, make a lot of money in business and give it to the church, and maybe you'll serve on a committee one day." That one statement wasted twenty years of my potential workplace ministry. Let me share some of the stories leading up to this statement and the birth of iWork4Him.

1979 was a challenging year for our nation economically, but it was a pivotal year in my life. As a thirteen-year-old, I got up the courage to ask my parents for $300 and permission to go to a summer youth conference with our church. The trip came at a time when I needed to make some life changes, and my parents agreed to write a check and let me go.

At the end of the conference, the speaker offered several challenges to the crowd. I knew I needed to go all-in with my faith. So that night, I stood up and committed my life to full-time Christian ministry. As a high school student, I gave my life work to God and assumed that I would someday be a youth pastor. Little did I know what God was going to teach me and how He would use my work.

A few years later, Martha and her family moved to Minnesota. We became fast friends and spent a lot of time together at church and leading Bible studies. After our first date, I knew we would marry. We discovered that we had attended that same youth conference in 1979 and made the same commitment to full-time Christian ministry. We assumed we would finish our four-year degrees and eventually go to seminary.

> I was absolutely being called into ministry—it just wasn't ministry in the four-walls church.

Martha and I got married in 1986. I completed my Computer Science degree, and a few semesters later, she earned a Management major and Accounting minor. We were ready to put our degrees into practice. We are entrepreneurs at heart and love sales, business, fixing problems, and answering customers' needs. I loved managing people and projects, and soon we started our own small business on the side.

I enrolled in seminary to stick to our commitment to God. Our senior pastor came to me and said, "Jim, there aren't enough laypeople out there within the church. We need more people who can volunteer. I also don't think you're cut out for full-time church ministry. You could never handle having 400 bosses. So why don't you stay in your insurance career and keep volunteering as a lay minister within the youth ministry?" After that, *lay minister* became like a swear word to me as I felt less valuable than a paid pastor.

I was absolutely being called into ministry—it just wasn't ministry in the four-walls church. Instead, God was calling me to minister in the marketplace ... if only my pastor had known how to communicate that to me!

The only context he had ever been taught was that if you have a call on your life, and you are a man, then your choices are to be a pastor or a foreign missionary. Period. Everyone else is simply called to fund them.

But what he was missing, and therefore what I was missing, made an impact on the first twenty years of my working life—and unfortunately, on the eternity of hundreds who didn't hear the gospel from me because I didn't know how to bring my faith to work. Based on my pastor's understanding, I thought my job was just to get people in the church's doors, where the church staff would do the rest.

I was devastated. For the previous ten years, Martha and I had thought that church ministry was in our future. I quit seminary, and we continued to volunteer. I didn't doubt that this message came from God, but it was hard news to take.

During that time in my life, I had two business mentors. I talked to them about the decision not to go to seminary. They were phenomenal people, who were also great businesspeople, but they didn't understand a connection between faith and work, either.

When I was about twenty-three years old, one of them said, "Business is business, and church is church. They have nothing to do with each other. So, make a lot of money in business and give it to the church, and maybe you'll serve on a committee one day."

That's how I was disabled as a Christian business guy. That message cut my feet out from under me. Multiple "Christian" businesspeople had mentored me to believe I should work all day long, make money to support the church, and volunteer my time for ministry at night and on weekends.

We loved doing youth ministry through the years, but this critical misinformation led me to believe, "Jim, your work doesn't matter. Just use it to make money." I had all these skills and education but didn't see how God could use them.

Through our twenties, we sold insurance and used cars together. We were successful businesspeople who loved our work and our employees. But we kept thinking we were doing these tasks to support our church. We ministered to many of our clients, but we lacked the mindset to connect our faith and work.

To grow our business, we purchased a chain of insurance agencies; at the same time, we committed to becoming debt-free. Through the biblical principles taught by Crown Financial Ministries, we determined we did not want debt to stand in the way of anything God would call us to do. So that year was full of changes, including moving to a smaller town, a smaller mortgage, and starting our hike up the debt-free mountain.

That same year, the doctor told Martha, "Your sinuses are a mess, and your circulation is bad. Most of your symptoms would improve if you moved somewhere warm near the saltwater. I would suggest Florida." Those were prophetic words.

We had only owned our hundred-year-old insurance agency for six months when the doctor shared his powerful suggestion to move. We spent the next four years preparing to sell the agency. We learned more about living a debt-free life during that time as God prepared our hearts to move to Florida.

> Theological circles still perpetuate the idea that there are "tiers" in the Kingdom of God.

I joked with my friends that at thirty-seven, I was planning my midlife crisis on my schedule. Little did I know that I must've made God laugh very hard with that statement. On my schedule and my terms. Right. :)

We moved to Florida and immediately joined a church and small group where we became fast friends with Bob and Deanna Keator. I was still trying to determine my next career move when Bob gave me the book *Halftime* by Bob Buford. The book taught me that I could pursue significance in my success.

I prayed, "Father, I've seen success. I would love to see success again, but I don't want to waste any more time. I want to pursue significance, and no matter what I do here in Florida, please show me the way to significance in my success."

If I had a hundred-dollar bill for every time a Jesus-follower came up to Martha and me and said, "I just want my life to make a difference. I am thinking about quitting my job and going to work at my church or a Christian nonprofit," I would be a wealthy man. So, where do Christians get the idea that their only hope for living in significance is found through working in a church or faith-based nonprofit?

For me, this idea was instilled from decades of listening to sermons praising those who followed Jesus into full-time ministry. Conversely, I never once heard that God gave us work as a blessing that can be used to bless others through the Great Commission.

Even today, theological circles around the globe continue to perpetuate the idea that there are "tiers" in the Kingdom of God. The top tier contains those called into full-time ministry in the roles of pastor or missionary. The rest of us? Tier two. It's how I felt—second string and second tier.

I was not alone. I have interviewed over two thousand people who have thought and said the same thing.

Being a teacher and a car dealer was at the top of my newly created career bucket list. Five weeks into a teaching job, I realized this would not be the last career move for me. But God used the teaching job to move me away from the car business to leave me open to the next opportunity. Each job was a turning point in my work and directed me closer to the start of iWork4Him.

My brother-in-law offered me a job that was a perfect fit and twice the pay. The only catch was he wanted me to start working for him right away. I told him I believed I needed to keep my teaching commitment until the end of the school year. So, until then, I was a teacher by day and risk manager by night.

iWork4Him Begins

My job as the IT operations and insurance risk manager of a construction project started full time in mid-May 2006. My daily commute to Orlando took 90 minutes in the morning and 120 minutes at night. I committed the morning drive to learn how to pray.

First, I started praying for my family, and then my four bosses, their spouses, and their families. Later, I added my co-workers and employees. I spent my morning commute praying through past hurts and bitterness and learning to intercede on behalf of those I love and serve.

My new job in Orlando used every skill I had developed in previous jobs. It was the best work of my life up to that time. Then my friend Bob, the same one who gave me the book *Halftime*, sent me a copy of the devotional *Today God Is First* (www.TodayGodisFirst.com) by Os Hillman. These devotionals taught me that my workplace was my place of ministry. I had never heard this before. I began sharing those devotionals with others in my office.

At forty years old, I had read through the Bible every year since my commitment at age thirteen, and *I had never heard from any pulpit or Bible study that my work mattered to God*. I learned I didn't need to work within the church's four walls to be in ministry. I began to realize that I was already in full-time Christian ministry.

I was in ministry in a job trailer on a construction site in Orlando. The transformation didn't happen overnight, but my understanding grew as I read these devotionals and other books about the connection between faith and work. My eyes were opening, and God was using me as a minister in my work.

It was 2008, and I had a dream job in the construction industry. It was a challenging year, and by the following spring, we shut down the job site. We closed the company by the end of 2009. The best job I ever had just disappeared. During these challenging months, I had the opportunity to pray with my bosses and staff many times. I took on the role of pastor in our workplace. It was such a great honor and privilege.

God had been teaching me about the Holy Spirit. I read *Forgotten God* by Francis Chan and was struck by his statement, and I paraphrase, "If you are successful using your natural gifts, talents, and abilities, then you get the credit. But if God uses you to do something unexplainable from your natural gifts, talents, and abilities, then God gets the credit." After reading this, I told the Lord I wanted a job like that. I asked Him to use me in a way where He gets the credit.

God was growing something new within me. I began studying how to disciple Christian businesspeople to understand their work's significance and uncovered God's maturing move in the marketplace, the Faith and Work Movement. I found many companies led by Jesus followers, Faith and Work ministries, and books on the subject.

I considered joining other organizations along the way, but God kept telling me to wait. I had an executive summary written and told the Lord that I would know He wanted me to move forward with this ministry when He gave me a name for it.

One evening I knew it was time to move forward when God gave me the name iWork4Him. I knew it was from God; it was direct, straightforward, and creative. Under the name iWork4Him, I could disciple four or five Christian businesspeople at a time but asked God how I could challenge thousands of people.

I had no platform to share. I wanted more impact than four or five people at a time. But I still didn't know what iWork4Him was. I just knew we were getting close to what God wanted for our lives. It had been almost ten years of God working on my heart and refining my job life.

In Tampa Bay, I had been part of a networking group that would later become the Christian Chamber of Commerce Tampa Bay. At our fifth anniversary gathering, I spoke on "Five ways to incorporate your faith in your workplace," and saw that it resonated with the audience.

I sat down in the room next to Deborah Roseman, the only person I didn't know, and she said that I needed to share that message on the radio. I thought she was crazy. But she repeated her statement, and I agreed to email her my executive summary for iWork4Him. Within the hour, she called me and reiterated the need to talk about iWork4Him on her radio station.

Martha and I met with Deborah to review the details and the costs involved to begin the one-hour radio show on Monday nights. I couldn't imagine spending money to talk on the radio, but as we walked out of the meeting, I told Martha, "This is the stupidest idea I've ever heard, but radio seems like the answer to our prayers. We prayed for a life of significance, a success that could only be attributed to God, and an opportunity to reach thousands with the iWork4Him message. I believe this is the answer to those prayers."

So, we said yes to radio and aired the first iWork4Him radio show on April 15, 2013. From the beginning, God gave me two significant directives to keep in mind as iWork4Him moved forward.

1. Don't reproduce the wheel.

2. Think big, very big, bigger than you can even think, ask, or imagine.

The first directive kept me from starting a ministry that probably already existed. Our job was to make existing Faith and Work–focused ministries famous and promote them to replicate. iWork4Him is to be a mouthpiece for the Faith and Work Movement.

> God was using the broadcast and podcast to challenge people to live out their faith at work.

The second directive from God is a constant challenge. I have never been described as a big thinker. I still don't know what God's bigger plan is, but He's done big things along the way, and I keep stretching myself to think bigger than I could ever ask or imagine (Ephesians 3:20).

For the first few years, we worked full-time jobs and hosted the iWork4Him Radio show five days a week. At one point, we formed a business partnership to support the expansion of iWork4Him. We spent quite a bit of time talking, praying, and fasting before we decided to move ahead with this partnership, but in the end, God said, "Enough! I want you to go all in. Stop trying to help Me. I will provide for you. Trust Me." We ended the business partnership and went all in.

God was using the broadcast and podcast to challenge people to live out their faith at work. We began traveling to conferences focused on the Faith and Work Movement. We interviewed Christian workplace believers from around the country, in big and small towns, capturing how they lived out their faith in their work.

Our travels also helped us make connections across the Kingdom of God. In many circles, we are called the mouthpiece for the Faith and Work Movement, where we focus on building collaboration and unity in the body of Christ. God has given us a bird's-eye view of what He is doing in the workplaces of Jesus followers all over the United States of America.

At the time of this writing, we are primarily digital, with our weekly thirty-minute podcast and show, as well as a one-minute show played on stations across the country. We took a summer sabbatical to finish three books: *iWork4Him*, *iRetire4Him*, and *sheWorks4Him*.

We are working on a digital-first marketing platform to advance iWork4Him nationally to challenge all 55 million Jesus followers in their work. To help them recognize that their workplace is their place of ministry, their assigned mission field.

God has been working on this story my whole life. He has used even hard mistakes to make me useable today and shown me that I am not less than. My work is valuable, and He wants to use me in my work to be a minister.

There is a solution to the twenty-year struggle I went through. God gave us the Cultural Mandate in Genesis to cultivate the earth and bring about flourishing for all. Then, in the Gospels, He gave us the Great Commandment to love Him and love others. And finally, in Matthew, He gave us the Great Commission to teach others what Jesus taught us. When these three come together in a workplace, God's true purpose for work is revealed: work as worship or "workship" (Avodah).

In the last decade, church attendance has declined. Even though people aren't going to church, they *are* going to work. This makes the workplace the richest mission field in America! So, how do we make sure the 55 million believers at work understand the significance of their work to the Kingdom of God?

In Matthew 28:19, Jesus said, "Go and produce disciples teaching them what I have taught you." He prepared His followers to transform the world through the power of His words and the power of the Holy Spirit living in them.

Today, our local churches should be doing the same thing: producing missionaries of *all types* for all kinds of professions. Sunday mornings (one hour of a 168-hour week) should be a prep session for the other 167 hours of ministry time in the community.

When every person in the pews realizes that God has placed them where they are on purpose and for a purpose (specifically, the purpose of being Jesus to all those around them), everything changes. Their job is no longer just a job; it's a calling to a mission field full of lost and hopeless people.

We have commissioning services for church pastors and foreign missionaries; how about a commissioning service for *everyone* who will leave the church building and impact the community?

As believers, everything about us should be changing (Romans 12:2), and everyone around us should be benefiting from our faith, whether they believe in Jesus or not. The early church lived out their faith in compelling ways throughout their local communities, and because of it, the entire Roman Empire was transformed! So, imagine what will happen when we unleash today's believers on the workplaces of America—there will be a transformation of our country and the world!

I had twelve employees, 1,500 clients, and twenty-five vendors. If just one person had spoken the truth to me about the size of my ministry and the potential impact I could have for the Kingdom of God as a business owner, I might have kept the business and made it a ministry platform for clients and employees.

If I had understood the purpose of my work and been fueled by Scripture and my pastor's teaching, I could have impacted the cities I operated in and been a blessing to my customers. But, unfortunately, *none* of that happened because *no one* ever told me I was on a mission field with enormous ministry potential.

Understanding God's view of work as worship leads to actions that naturally result in ministry. You see, your workplace, it's your mission field. And in that mission field, you and me, we may be the only Jesus our coworkers, employees, or bosses may ever meet. The job you hold, the work you do, and the people you work with—none of that is by chance. The people you work with need to meet Jesus, and you may be their only chance.

With this understanding, our actions can change the world.

Questions for Reflection and Application

1. With so much of the New Testament and the ministry of the Jesus occurring in the context of the marketplace. Why is it that we have such a persistent sacred/secular and church/ marketplace dichotomy? How can we rectify this?

2. The author writes, "Sunday mornings (one hour of a 168-hour week) should be a prep session for the other 167 hours of ministry time in the community." He then issues the challenge, "So, imagine what will happen when we unleash today's believers on the workplaces of America." What do you think could happen in your community, and what changes could take place?

Jim Brangenberg is an established leader in the faith and work movement and has over twenty years of experience as an entrepreneur and business owner. In 2013, God called him and his wife, Martha, to begin the iWork4Him Talk Show, where they have had the privilege of challenging thousands across the globe with the simple message that your workplace is your mission field.

A natural relator, Jim has arranged and interviewed over 3,000 CEOs, business owners, authors, and Christ-followers in the workplace on the iWork4Him and iRetire4Him shows. In addition, he and Martha have co-authored a series of collaborative books, *iWork4Him, sheWorks4Him,* and *iRetire4Him.*

Jim and Martha have been married for 35+ years and have three grown children and six grandchildren. When Jim isn't interviewing, speaking, or mentoring, he and Martha lead marriage retreats and tackle DIY projects together.

13
Two Pillars
Paul Cuny

1 Kings 7:21 *Thus he set up the pillars at the porch of the nave; and he set up the right pillar and named it Jachin, and he set up the left pillar and named it Boaz.*

King Solomon was building the first Temple of the Lord. The details of this Temple were drawn up by Solomon's father, King David, with the prophet Nathan. It was in David's heart to build this Temple for the Lord, but he was judged to have shed too much blood, so the task was given to his son, Solomon.

The Porch of the Nave was a covered entrance to this magnificent structure. Two massive, identical bronze columns were set at the entrance of the Porch for support. Scholars say they were set before the entrance as "pillars of witness" or "pillars of remembrance."

Because the prophet Nathan was involved in the plans for the Temple, we can be assured that God had His hand in the details. Why would the Lord want these pillars so prominently displayed? What did God want us to remember? What were they a "witness" to? Who were the two men these massive columns were named for? Why did they have their names on these columns?

Each carving, every detail of the Temple, had significance to the priests and Levites and the people. Why were these two identical bronze pillars set at the entrance of the Temple, so that every worshipper would be called to "remembrance"?

Who Were These Men?

The first pillar was named Jachin (Hebrew for "Yahweh will establish"). He was an honored priest during the reign of King David. It was certainly appropriate for a pillar supporting the Porch of the Nave to be named after a renowned priest. However, we will focus on the second pillar named Boaz (Hebrew for "In Yahweh is the King's strength").

Boaz was a wealthy landowner from Bethlehem. I understood Boaz to be a successful farmer, a respected businessman, and a leader in his city, as well as an ancestor of Jesus. However, why have a pillar named after a farmer/ businessman in the most important structure in Jewish history?

I must confess to some unspoken skepticism as I studied these two pillars. I thought about the "Bricks of Faith" concept, even in Solomon's day! "Buy 100 Bricks of Faith for the building of the Temple and your name will be placed in a small plaque. Buy 10,000 Bricks of Faith and we will give you a massive bronze column at the entrance with your name on it!"

As I read these verses, I pictured Solomon going to this wealthy farmer/businessman and saying, "Boaz, if you 'donate' a large amount of shekels to the Temple, we will have your name inscribed on the pillar at the entrance of the temple. Then everyone will remember you and the offerings you gave."

Pastors know that on occasion, marketplace people like to have their names engraved on things. The more "bricks of faith" we buy, the bigger our names get carved on stones for all to see. While I believe this is the antithesis of true Kingdom leadership, I confess after reading these verses, I thought to myself, "Boaz must have paid a great deal for this massive bronze pillar to carry his name."

Boaz: A Man of Integrity

However, my initial thoughts and skepticism about Boaz were completely wrong. Boaz was not a contemporary of Solomon, but he lived almost 250 years earlier. He was Solomon's great-great-great-grandfather. So revered and honored was this successful farmer/businessman that we are still talking about him thousands of years later. He was a godly man of such integrity, honor, and high moral character that the Lord chose him to be an ancestor of the Messiah.

Boaz was a true representative of a Biblical culture or business by expressing kindness to an alien and affording privileges to Ruth the Moabite even though she was not a Jew. Deuteronomy 14:29: "The Levite, because he has no portion or inheritance among you, and the alien, the orphan and the widow who are in your town, shall come and eat and be satisfied, in order that the LORD your God may bless you in all the work of your hand which you do."

Boaz became Ruth's "kinsman redeemer," a term used to describe the work of Jesus on the cross.

The Awakening

If you serve God in the Sunday morning pulpits of the world, you might not be aware of a global awakening that is taking place. The reason is that this awakening is taking place outside the walls of the church house. This awakening, this move of God, is emerging in the streets of commerce and the halls of government, and it is global.

This awakening is a tangible expression of the reality that God desires to extend His influence through His people Monday through Saturday. Many religious leaders have been expecting this for some time. It has been labeled by some as "the saints move."

I do not know about the labels, but I have seen this awakening growing in many of the nations I have traveled to over the last twenty years. This movement is not a voice of competition with the church, but it will cause the glory of God to be manifested in the church in an even greater way.

> God uses men and women who are committed to His ways and His plans, no matter the cost.

You may ask, where are they? The men and women who are beginning to experience this awakening and those who are leading it are faithfully sitting in the congregations of churches around the world. They are most likely in your church, and they will need your understanding, your endorsement and, most of all, your friendship.

We know that God uses men and women who are committed to His ways and His plans, no matter the cost. Those who are embracing this movement may not speak from the same pulpits you stand in, but they do have pulpits and they do preach the message of the Kingdom.

They stand in their pulpits at work on Monday morning and the message of the Kingdom is preached in the way they conduct their lives, their businesses, or their responsibilities because that is a reflection of Jesus to those they encounter. The influence of the Kingdom of God on national cultures can be extended through these faithful men and women who carry the passion for God, the calling, and His anointing to bring the change that God desires.

Misunderstanding the Sacred/Secular

A sacred calling is not simply our response to God's call as a missionary, a pastor, or an evangelist, but a response to His specific plan for our lives—whatever plan that may be. He is the ultimate strategist, and the Kingdom of God must have influencers and ambassadors in all spheres of society, as well as the church. I can provide many examples of how this works in the 21st century, but one that illustrates this is my European friend.

He is one of the world's leading economists. He had such a passion for God at a young age that he was planning for seminary when God spoke to him, "I want you to study economics." This Spirit-filled lover of God was given a revelation of a "new economic theory" based on Leviticus 25.

That economic theory is now being taught in major universities around the world. It is possible for men and women to receive that sacred calling to business, government, vocational ministry or, in my friend's case, economics, and still serve the sacred purposes of God in our generation. The Scripture tells us that is so.

The prophet Daniel was a top government leader for three heathen kings. Yet, he was also a servant of God who was given a divine revelation that is still unfolding in our generation!

We all know Nehemiah was a wine taster for the King of Persia. However, after receiving the assignment from God to go to Jerusalem, he was appointed as the Governor of Judah by the king. And because of God's anointing on His agent, he organized the remarkable rebuilding of the walls of the city that had been down for 142 years.

Men and women like this, even today, seem to have a never-ending flow of the revelation of God to solve societal problems, and such was Nehemiah. In Nehemiah 7:5, by the revelation of God, he restructured society the way God originally intended it. Under his leadership—a leader with a sacred calling—created the conditions for the great revival which occurred in collaboration with Ezra the priest (Nehemiah 8:1-9).

Then there is the prophet Amos. If you casually read the verse in Amos 1:1, you would get the picture that he was just this humble shepherd from the Southern Kingdom who was a prophet to the Northern Kingdom. However, the Hebrew word for shepherd is *noqed,* and it is only used twice in the entire Bible. The other time it is used it describes a Moabite king named Mesha. It was said of King Mesha that he had 750,000 sheep and used to tithe the wool of 100,000 sheep annually to King Solomon.

The publisher of the Jewish Study Bible (Old Testament only) brought together forty of the world's leading Rabbinical scholars to research and produce this study Bible for Jews. This is their note for Amos 1:1: "The verse tells the readers that Amos was a herdsman, a sheep, and cattle breeder. As such, Amos was a relatively wealthy man. He was not a poor shepherd as is at times erroneously claimed."[18] Amos was a businessman!

---

[18] The Jewish Study Bible, Adele Berlin and Marc Zvi Brettler – Editors; Michael Fishbane, Consulting Editor, Jewish Publication Society, TANAKH Translation, page 1177 Oxford University Press, Inc., Oxford, New York Copyright 2004.

No one reading this book can say that these men—men who wrote a book of the Bible that we hold so dear, men who were committed to the purposes of God for their generation and beyond, and men who heard His voice and at great personal risk challenged the existing culture of the day—were in secular work. Each of them was positioned by God to extend His influence and plans in their generation, and we are reading about their exploits still today.

How Does This Help You?

What does all this mean for you as a pastor when you gather your congregation next Sunday morning? I want to offer a few observations that may help you identify and minister to these men and women who are leaders or emerging leaders in this move of God. Remember, we are talking about men and women with a passion for Jesus and their specific calling.

- **The Church**: They are not in competition with you and therefore, you have no reason to view them with suspicion or keep them at a distance. We know God loves the local church in all its expressions, so you will find that the marketplace leaders God sends to you love what God loves! They are sacred allies with a different calling, but they are allies, nonetheless. Does that mean they will be in church every time the doors open? Probably not, but do not judge them for that because their God-given assignments are outside the church house.

- **Isolation**: Pastors know well the isolation that comes with leadership. To effectively minister to those marketplace leaders in your church, you must understand that the men and women who are positioned by God to extend His influence in the marketplace experience this same kind of isolation. I was part of a pastors' conference some years ago and heard one speaker after another speak about the isolation that they experienced in ministry. They spoke about the isolation pastors experience as unique. Yet I can assure you that this isolation is not unique to pastors. You certainly have different pressures that come with your office, but I have personally experienced this, and have met Kingdom leaders all over the world who experience some level of isolation because of their calling. The answer for all of us is safe friendship with peer-level men and women with a like heart for the things of God and similar calling—not necessarily the identical calling.

- **Motivation**: Pastors correctly view their pulpits as a way to motivate others to a life of Godliness in Christ Jesus. For some in your congregation, this is certainly true. However, the marketplace leaders in your church who have a clear vision for the assignments God has set before them do not need your motivation because He has already motivated them. You have to treat them differently than those who look to you for motivation. Identify them, come alongside them, and help them in their journey.

- **Revival/Reform**: Many church leaders I know have a heart for revival because it touches the heart of men. Revival happens when the finger of God touches an individual's life. Revival can dramatically change our perspective and life's purpose, but revival is not the goal—it is the foundation. Revival is personal; reform is cultural. Revival is the beginning of the cultural reform that the Kingdom of God can bring to society. The real evidence of revival in a city or nation is found in the streets of commerce and the halls of government, when God uses these men and women who are touched by revival to influence others for righteousness in all aspects of society. It is entirely possible that the marketplace leaders in your church see their responsibilities before the Lord as reformers called to extend Kingdom influence in business, or government, medicine, education, the military, or any other sphere of society.

- **Vision**: We can only see what God enables us to see. He is the one who gives the eyesight and the vision. Most church leaders see the local church, or in some cases the church in the city or the nation. You will find that those marketplace leaders who are destined to bring a Kingdom influence have been given a view outside the walls of the church house. They may not serve on your elder board or teach Sunday school, but they will have a heart to serve because this is the key characteristic for all Kingdom leadership, whether inside the church or outside the church.

- **Commissioning**: Church leaders frequently commission or ordain pastors and missionaries publicly, but have you ever commissioned business leaders, medical students, or government leaders who have the call of God to perhaps do what Amos, Daniel, or Nehemiah did? If you believe that one group has a sacred responsibility, and the other is in secular work, then the answer is probably not. I'm not suggesting a casual approach to something as sacred as commissioning or ordination, but after proper evaluation of the life and calling, your validation will do wonders not only for your church but also for the lives they will affect.

The Mythical Ladder

Some church leaders mistakenly promote the concept that God has this mythical ladder we must climb to "really be used by God." They may subtly communicate the idea that the very bottom rung of this mythical ladder is the marketplace (business, government, etc.), which is often referred to as "secular work" or "working for money."

To reach the top rung of this mythical ladder, which represents the only legitimate service to God, we must leave the marketplace and become pastors or missionaries. When you promote this kind of thinking, it produces two misconceptions for the hearers.

The First Misconception

The first misconception is you will subtly communicate God's involvement in their work life is minimal; therefore, accountability to Him is also minimal. If God is not that involved, then it does not matter if marketplace leaders lack integrity from time to time.

If He only becomes fully engaged with the "sacred" and marketplace people are at the bottom rung of this mythical ladder ("secular"), they are more or less left to their own devices with marginal involvement from God.

This misconception produces people in your church who blend in with the world around them. If we are true followers of Jesus Christ, this is unacceptable, and the Scripture dispels this misconception.

Colossians 3:23 says, "Whatever you do, do your work heartily, as for the Lord rather than for men..." Everything they do during the workday is holy to the Lord. It does not matter whether we pastor a church or clean a toilet, whether we are a missionary, an ambassador, or a ditch digger.

According to Colossians 3, it is all holy to Him. He cares about it all; from how hard we work, to our punctuality and integrity, to the respect of those in authority over us. We represent Him to the world Monday through Saturday. He is fully engaged, all the time, in everything we do, whether it is the worship service at church or leading a stockholders' meeting at a Fortune 500 company. He is looking for an exhibition of our character (His character in us) in all these things.

The Second Misconception

The second misconception you communicate is that we must move from "secular work" to "sacred work" to get to the top of this mythical ladder. I remember after the first segment at one of my MarketPlace Leadership Conferences in El Salvador, a pastor in his fifties came up to me and he was crying. He told me about his deep desire to serve God and minister to people.

He said he had been a businessman for many years but had a business failure some years ago. He thought that this failure meant that he was probably doing the wrong thing and God wanted him to be a pastor. He thought it would not be possible to serve God as a businessman, so he went into the professional ministry.

He was embraced by some ministry colleagues as one who had finally seen the light, and eventually became a pastor of a church. Even though he was a pastor, he continued this love for and deep interest in business. He confessed to me that he had struggled to find fulfillment and effectiveness in this role as pastor.

> When God calls us to a role, whatever that role is, we have been divinely equipped by Him for that specific role.

He said the Lord had spoken to him during that first segment of our conference that he was never "called" to this role of a pastor, but God had indeed "called" him to business. He told me that he now understood that he was meant to serve God with the same zeal and passion in business. He raised his hands to Heaven, wept for joy, and said, "¡Gloria a Dios!"

God Knows How Many Pastors the World Needs

The world needs pastors and marketplace people need pastors. The Kingdom will not function without them. They care for our souls and, by God's design, they have a special place in every culture. But God knows how many pastors the world needs, so He equips just the right number for every generation. If you are not equipped emotionally and spiritually to be a pastor, you will have a very difficult job trying to fulfill that role over the long term.

The broader view is that God's people, who need the care of one of His pastors, will not get what they need. You will eventually flourish when you find the role you have been divinely equipped to fulfill, whether that is as a pastor, a housewife, or an entrepreneur.

Many people in the marketplace, who have the heart to serve God, find themselves confused about these issues. We do not seem to be getting the message to the body of believers worldwide, that it is perfectly appropriate and necessary for us to serve God in the marketplace if this is God's role for us. The issue for all of us is, "What is our role?" When God calls us to a role, whatever that role is, we have been divinely equipped by Him for that specific role. Only in that role will we become most effective and find lasting fulfillment.

The Understanding Gap

What is God's model? Many marketplace people are not quite sure where they fit in this Kingdom of God. We thrive in a world of government or business, yet there is a desire to please the Lord with our lives. How could God care about any occupation other than "real" ministry? How do we find our place? How do we bridge this "understanding gap" to be released to do what we are called to do, whatever that calling may be?

This awakening I speak about is a reflection of God giving understanding to both church and marketplace leaders. At the same time, He is activating people in congregations with strategies to bring Jesus Christ to the world in unique ways. Marketplace people are being positioned to transform and lead businesses and governments.

The creativity of God will be expressed through entrepreneurs and marketplace leaders in your congregations. Financial resources usually come with God's strategies to bring the Kingdom to cities, regions, and nations.

Divine Order

All of this can be summarized as a question of Divine Order. God gave us a perfect picture of what this looked like in the Books of Ezra and Nehemiah. Ezra, the renowned priest who "...set his heart to study the law of the LORD and to practice it, and to teach His statutes and ordinances in Israel." (Ezra 7:10) was sent to Jerusalem fourteen years before Nehemiah. His responsibility was to bring Divine Order to the Temple. Like many of you, Ezra saw the devastation and the oppression of the people in his generation, yet his assignment was the Temple.

Nehemiah was also sent to Jerusalem to bring Divine Order. His responsibility was to bring Divine Order outside the walls of the rebuilt Temple to the City of Jerusalem and Judah. Ezra and Nehemiah were contemporaries who were both sent by God to do different things. They worked together, and the results were an expression of the blessing of God on that generation.

A beautiful picture of this collaboration is found in Nehemiah 8. After rebuilding the walls, a podium was built for the reading of the Law. The notable omission from those listed on the platform in Nehemiah. He understood where his place was and that was with the people listening to the reading of the Law by Ezra and the priests and Levites. This is an example of true Kingdom leadership for us in the 21st century. May the Lord raise up those men and women in your churches who are the Nehemiahs of this generation!

Questions for Reflection and Application

1. The author ponders the fact that a pillar in the temple was named after Boaz, a farmer and businessman. What role do you think businesspeople should play in the Kingdom?

2. The author differentiates between revival and reformation. He says the real evidence of revival is seen in (reformation) in the streets of commerce and the halls of government? If you had to rate revival (individual and in the church) and reformation (impacting the culture) on a scale of 1 (nonexistent) to 10 (ablaze with the transformational move of God), how would you rate your church and community?

3. The author describes a mythical ladder of importance wherein one "must move from 'secular work' to 'sacred work' to get to the top of this mythical ladder." Is there anything in your systems or messaging that reinforces this ladder concept?

Paul L. Cuny is President of MarketPlace Leadership International, Chairman of the International Christian Chamber of Commerce USA (ICCC-USA), North American Regional Director of ICCC, and Steering Committee Member of the Economic Summit. His compelling desire is to help men and women grow in the applied revelation of the economic principles of the Bible in daily life.

A background as an entrepreneur and business owner has provided a platform from which to speak to leaders and professionals and then challenge them to walk in the fullness of the Kingdom and to pursue the presence of God in professional life. Paul is ordained and commissioned as ambassador of the Gospel of the Kingdom.

Paul Cuny is recognized internationally as a speaker on God's principles of economics and leadership. He has spoken at conferences and churches in Africa, Europe, South and Central America, the Caribbean, and the United States. Paul emphasizes the practical application of the Biblical systems of the Kingdom in the 21st-century professional life by moving closer to God and living life in the power of the Spirit.

Paul is a teacher with a prophetic anointing for the nations. He is one of the founding leadership team members of the Economic Summit which includes some of the world's top economists, government, business, and Christian leaders who are developing new economic paradigms for nations based on the Scripture.

Paul has authored many articles in prominent international publications and is the author of two books: *Secrets of the Kingdom Economy*, which is published in five languages, and *Nehemiah People*, which is published in three languages.

Paul has a calling as "...a friend of kings." He has served as a friend, advisor, and prayer partner to sitting presidents as well as top-level business, government, and political leaders in the nations of the world.

INDEX

#

1 Corinthians 65
1 Kings 211
1 Peter
    1 65
    2 .... 59, 65
    3 62
1 Timothy 18
100 Leadership Nuggets
    Robinson, David 160
10x Catalyst Groups 189
2 Peter 62
2 Thessalonians 65
50 Leadership Keys That Work
    Robinson, David 160

A

Aaron 49
Abel 26
Abominable Snowman, The
    Robinson, David 160
Abraham 71, 144
Acton University 93
Acts
    9 65
    17 148
    19 .... 24, 32
Adam 9–10, 26, 60, 71
Alexander, Ashish and Vishal Mangalwadi

This Book Changed Everything: The Bible's Amazing Impact on Our World
    63

AdultPreneurs 88–89
Amalek 47, 49
Amalekites 47, 56
Amos 216, 220
Amos
    1 216
    9 187
Andrew 65
Anointed for Business
    Silvoso, Ed 24–25, 36, 123
apostle 31, 36, 65–66, 71, 148, 151, 164–166, 189
Apostle Paul 17, 24, 32, 65, 147, 151, 162
Apostle Peter 24, 59–60, 62, 65, 96
Ark of the Covenant 33
Aslan Group Publishing
    Hillman, Os 185
At Work on Purpose 129, 131, 133–134, 136
ATS Murdock Report 162

B

Barna Research Group 82, 92
Barna: The State of Pastors
    110
Bending the Twig

Rudd, Augustin G. 145
Benedict, Jason
........................59–75, 127, 136
Benedict, Kimberly 75
Benham, David................5–21
    Benham Real Estate 5
    Expert Ownership 21
    HGTV........................7–8, 21
Benham, Jason.................5–21
    Benham Real Estate 5
    Expert Ownership 21
    HGTV........................7–8, 21
Bethel Church
    Vallotton, Kris 192–193
Bezalel.......................... 33–34
Bible, The Holy 5–8, 13, 17, 18, 21, 27, 30–33, 47, 61, 63, 67, 71, 113, 141, 143–145, 154, 157, 161–162, 180–181, 183, 198, 203, 216–217, 226
BIZNISTRY: Transforming Lives through Enterprise
    Proudfit, Chuck 137
Boaz..................... 211–213, 226
Bonnke, Reinhard 56
Brangenberg, Jim
.... 197–210
Brangenberg, Martha
.....................199–201, 205, 210
Brown, Michael
    Michael's Transportation
    ....25, 28, 33, 35
Buford, Bob
    Halftime..................201, 203
Bush, George W. 133

Business As Ministry
.........................120–121, 123

C

C12 Group 119–120, 189
Cain...................................... 26
calling 2–3, 10, 64–65, 73, 83. 87, 118–119, 121–122, 125, 127, 134, 146–147, 149–150, 156–157, 159, 161–163, 169, 181, 183, 185, 199, 208, 215–218, 220, 223, 227, 243, 247
Catchim, Tim and Alan Hirsch
    Permanent Revolution: Apostolic Imagination and Practice for the 21st Century Church, The
   165
CEO Forum 189
Cessationism 146
Chambers, Oswald
    My Utmost for His Highest
   180
Chan, Francis
    Forgotten God................ 204
Chapman, Gary
    Five Languages of Appreciation for the Workplace, The 160
    Paul White.....................160
Christian Business Men's Committee (CBMC)
.................................119, 189
Christian Chamber of Commerce Tampa Bay 205
Christian Outreach Centre
.... 50

Church for Monday 92, 97, 99

Church for Monday: Equipping Believers for Mission at Work

Papazov, Svetlana
.... 110–111, 162

Church Multiplication Network 93

Cincinnati Christian University

Proudfit, Chuck 137

Citywide Workplace Ministry in a Box

Proudfit, Chuck 137

Clapham Sect 2

Colossians

1 26

3 221

Commissioned 189, 196

Kramer, James

Connecting Businessmen to Christ (CBMC) 177

Constantine, Emperor 146

Convene 189

conventus 31–32, 36

Cracknell, Kevin................. 15

CrossFit.............................. 18

Crown Financial Ministries 200

Cuny, Paul 211–227

Nehemiah People 227

Secrets of the Kingdom Economy 227

D

Daniel 215, 220

David............ 8, 60, 71, 211–212

Deuteronomy

8............................... 144, 194

14 213

Divine Order.....................224

Dominion-Stewardship
.... 115, 117, 123–124

E

Ecclesiastes

5 115

Egypt.......................47–48, 188

ekklesia............ 29–33, 36, 188

Ekklesia 23, 29

Silvoso, Ed

Eldred, Ken

God Is at Work 123

Empower Church 57

Enoch 71

Entrepreneurial Engineering Program

Melton, Douglas 79

Ephesians

1.......................26, 62, 65, 116

2...............................65, 166

3 206

4 ......65–66, 115, 125, 140–141, 147–148, 155, 157–159, 164–165, 183

5 164

Esau 47

Evangel 110

Eve 26

Every Good Endeavor

Keller, Timothy............. 122

Exodus
- 4 48
- 12 188
- 17 47–49
- 18 41

Expert Ownership
- Benham, David 22
- Benham, Jason 22

Ezra 216, 224

Ezra
- 7 224

F

Faith and Public School Partnership Prototype ... 85

Faith and Work Movement 204, 206–207, 210

Fellowship of Companies for Christ International 119

Five Languages of Appreciation for the Workplace, The
- Chapman, Gary and Paul White 160

five-fold functions 164

Forgotten God
- Chan, Francis 204

Full Gospel Businessmen's Fellowship International 119, 178
- Shakarian, Demos 178

G

Garden of Eden 9, 69, 71

Gates of Hades 28, 31

Genesis 207
- 3 .... 10, 71
- 12 18
- 22 140–142
- 24 142

Gibbs, Joe 19

Global Thrive Index 189

God, 5–14, 16–21, 23–26, 28, 30– 36, 40–43, 45–49, 54–57, 59–62, 64–66, 68–71, 75, 77, 79–88, 90, 92, 94–95, 97–101, 103, 105, 107, 109, 113–118, 121–126, 131–133, 136, 139–145, 147–150, 152–159, 164, 167, 169, 172–187–173, 177, 179–186, 187–188, 190, 192, 194, 197–210, 211, 213–224, 226–227

God Is at Work
- Eldred, Ken 123

Graham, Billy 10

Great Commandment
- 94, 208

Great Commission 79, 81, 94, 127, 184, 187, 190, 202, 208

Great Oaks Institute
- Proudfit, Chuck 137

Great Transfer of Wealth, The
- Wagner, C. Peter 188

H

Haley, Alex
- *Roots* 170

Halftime
- Buford, Bob 201, 203

Halftime Institute 177

Halverson, Richard C.
  Walk With God Between Sundays....................... 155
Harvest Evangelism
  Silvoso, Ed....................... 36
Heaven in Business........... 189
Hillman, Os........ 177–186, 203
  Aslan Group Publishing
  .... 185, 189,
  Marketplace Leaders
  .... 177, 185, 200
  TGIF: Today God Is First
  .... 185–186, 203
Hillman, Pamela 186
Hiram, King................... 34
Hirsch, Alan and Tim Catchim
  Permanent Revolution: Apostolic Imagination and Practice for the 21st Century Church, The
 165
History of European Morals from Augustus to Charlemagne
  Lecky, W. E. H................. 94
Hodgson, David 33–57
Holy Spirit 23–25, 33–36, 60, 79, 85, 96, 130, 140, 149, 167–169, 172, 189–190, 196, 204, 208
Humphrey, Kent
  Shepherding Horses........ 163
Hur....................................... 49

I

Idle in the Marketplace at the Eleventh Hour
  Robinson, David 160
In His Steps
  Sheldon, Charles............. 117
Influence magazine 110
International Christian Chamber of Commerce (ICCC)............................. 119
iRetire4Him............... 207, 210
Isaac................................... 47
Isaiah ...., 143, 168
Isaiah
  6....................................... 168
  58...35
  59.................................... 143
Israel 30, 47, 49, 65, 187–188, 224
Israelites 47, 187
iWork4Him
  .... 197, 202–207, 210

J

Jachin............................211-212
James 65, 96
Jeremiah
  29................................. 66, 79
Jesus Christ 13–14, 16, 23, 25–33, 35, 56–57, 60–62, 64–66, 70–72, 79–80, 82–83, 86, 91–96, 98–99, 101, 104, 113, 117–119, 124–126, 129, 136, 139–141, 143–144, 147–149, 151–153, 163–164, 166, 168, 171, 177–183–184, 188, 192,

197, 201–202, 204, 207–210, 212–214, 217–218, 221, 223

Jethro
    Midianite priest 41

Jewish Study Bible 216

John 65, 69, 96, 152

John
    1 80
    5 82
    13 .... 95, 113
    20 60

John the Baptist 152

Joshua 48–49

K

KBA 189

Keator, Bob 201

Keator, Deanna 201

Keller, Timothy
    Every Good Endeavor 122

Kern Family Foundation
    Melton, Douglas 79

KidPreneurs
    Papazov, Svetlana 77, 88, 90,

King Mesha 216

King of Persia 215

Kingdom Investors (KI)
    .... 38, 40, 57, 189

Kingdom of God 28, 30–32, 55, 98–99, 105, 107, 145, 201, 207–208, 219, 223

Klepacki, Kenny 191–192

Kramer, James 187–1962

L

Late Great Planet Earth, The
    117

Leading Hearts 110

Lecky, W. E. H.
    History of European Morals from Augustus to Charlemagne 94

Left Behind 117

Legatum 189

Levites 211, 224, 245

Leviticus
    25 215

Liberty University 5

Life Changers Legacy
    Hillman, Pamela 186

Lifeforming Leadership Coaching
    Umidi, Joseph 175

Luke
    4 166
    7 152
    10 24
    19 .... 26–27, 95, 192–193

Luther, Martin 63
    Von Bora, Katarina 63

M

Made to Flourish 93

Mammon 46–47, 190, 194

Mangalwadi, Vishal and Ashish Alexander
    This Book Changed Everything: The Bible's Amazing Impact on Our World
    63–64

Marketplace Leaders
    Hillman, Os 177, 185, 189

MarketPlace Leadership Conference
    Cuny, Paul 221, 226

Matthew 225
Matthew
   4 65
   5 .... 61, 70, 113, 156,
   7 70
   10 126
   16 151
   20 146–147
   25 .... 57, 106, 193
   28 .... 60, 113, 140
McNeal, Reggie 98
Melton, Douglas 79
   Entrepreneurial
      Engineering Program
   Kern Family Foundation
Michael's Transportation
   Brown, Michael
       .... 25, 28, 33, 35
Midianites 41, 187
Mission2Monday 132
missioneering 12–15,
       17–19, 21
Monday morning
   assignment 67, 72
Mosaix 93
Moses 33–34, 41, 47–49, 71
Mulford, John E. 113–128
My Utmost for His Highest
   Chambers, Oswald 195

N

Nathan 211
National Christian Foundation 189
Nehemiah ... 215–216, 220, 224
Nehemiah
   7 216

   8 .... 216, 224
Nehemiah Foundation 137
Nehemiah People
   Cuny, Paul 227
New Jerusalem 61, 69
Noah 71
None Dare Call It Education
   Stormer, John A. 145

O

Oikos 188

P

Paladin Corporation 54
Paladin Group 56–57
Papazov, Svetlana
    .... 77–111, 162
   Church for Monday
       .... 110–111, 162
Patel, Neil 101
Permanent Revolution: Apostolic Imagination and Practice for the 21st Century Church, The
   Hirsch, Alan and Tim Catchim 165
Peter 24, 59–60, 62, 65, 96
Philippians
   2 171
Philippines 14–15
Pinnacle Forum 177, 189
Pneuma33 Creative
   Kramer, James 196
Porch of the Nave 211–212
Possessing the Gates of Your Enemy
   Robinson, David 160

Proudfit, Chuck......... 129–137
   BIZNISTRY: Transforming Lives through Enterprise 137
   Citywide Workplace Ministry in a Box...............137
Proverbs
   13 188
Pruett, Trent...................... 16
Psalm
   2........................ 141
   90 181

R

Real Life Center for Entrepreneurial and Leadership Excellence............88
Real Life Church
   ....77, 87, 88, 91, 110
   Papazov, Svetlana
Real Life Entrepreneurs... 102
Real Life incubator............ 89
Real Life KidPreneurs
   ....77, 87, 90
   Papazov, Svetlana
Real Life Scorecard 101
Regent Center for Entrepreneurship....................127
Regent University
   .... 75, 127, 164, 175, 185
Rephidim 47
Revelation
   5........................ 116
   22...................... 69
Rhodesia 51, 53, 56
Robinson, David........ 139–160
   100 Leadership Nuggets 160
   50 Leadership Keys That Work 160
   Abominable Snowman, The 160
   Idle in the Marketplace at the Eleventh Hour 160
   Possessing the Gates of Your Enemy 160
Rod of God 47–49, 56
Romans
   8........................116
   12...................... 209
   14.......................190
Roots
   Haley, Alex......................170
Rudd, Augustin G.
   Bending the Twig 145
Russia.............................. 51–52
Ruth the Moabite 213

S

Safe Haven
   Pruett, Amy 19
   Pruett, Trent....................19
Saint Bonaventure 180
salt and light
   .... 61, 70, 113, 132, 142
Schmidt, Alvin J.
   Under the Influence 62
Secrets of the Kingdom Economy
   Cuny, Paul 227
Selous Scouts 51, 56
Septuagint 143
Shakarian, Demos
   Full Gospel Businessmen's Fellowship International 177

Sheldon, Charles
   In His Steps 117
Shepherding Horses
   Humphrey, Kent .... 16.
Sherman, Doug
   Your Work Matters to God 122
sheWorks4Him 207, 210
Signatry, The 189
Silvoso, Ed 23–36, 123
Sivarajan, Ajit 16
SKILLSOURCE
   Proudfit, Chuck 136–137
Smith Family Foundation
   137
Solomon
   .... 33–34, 60, 211–213, 216
Solomon's Temple 60, 211
spiritual covering 37–57
Stanley McChrystal
   Team of Teams 133–134
Stormer, John A.
   None Dare Call It Education 145
SweetBridge 189

T

Team of Teams
   McChrystal, Stanley 133–134
TeenPreneurs 88
TGIF: Today God Is First
   Hillman, Os 185–186
This Book Changed Everything: The Bible's Amazing Impact on Our World
   Vishal Mangalwadi and Ashish Alexander 63

Transform Our World Network
   Silvoso, Ed 36
Transformational Coaching: Bridge Building that Impacts, Connects, and Advances the Ministry and the Marketplace
   Umidi, Joseph 96
TrustBridge 189

U

Umidi, Joseph 96, 161–175
   Transformational Coaching: Bridge Building that Impacts, Connects, and Advances the Ministry and the Marketplace
   96
   Lifeforming Leadership Coaching 1759
Under the Influence
   Schmidt, Alvin J. 62

V

Vallotton, Kris
   Bethel Church 192–193
Van Duzer, Jeff
   Why Business Matters to God 10
Virgin Mary 35
Von Bora, Katarina
   Luther, Martin 63

W

Wagner, C. Peter
   Great Transfer of Wealth, The 188

Walk With God Between Sundays
   Halverson, Richard C. 155

Wanlapa.................. 24, 33–35

Westminster Reformed Presbyterian Church 125

White, Paul

  Five Languages of Appreciation for the Workplace, The 160

  Why Business Matters to God
   Van Duzer, Jeff 10

Wilberforce, William 2

Wimber, John 166

Wittenberg 63

World Changer Foundation
   Kramer, James 196

worldchangers 59–75

Y

Your Work Matters to God
   Sherman, Doug 122

Z

Zacchaeus 27, 95–97

Zambia 51–53

Zimbabwe 56

Made in the USA
Middletown, DE
02 July 2023

34415474R00139